CREATED IN THE IMAGE OF GOD

CREATED IN THE IMAGE OF GOD

A Scriptural Exploration of Creation, God's Divine
Character, and Our Sin and Need for a Savior

ROGER RICHEY

*inspire*books

Published by Inspire Books
www.inspire-books.com

Print ISBN: 978-1-961065-10-9
e-book ISBN: 978-1-961065-11-6

Library of Congress Control Number: 2024905826

Printed in the United States

It would be impossible to thank every person who has had an impact on my Christian walk. But I would like to thank my parents, especially my mother, Faye Richey, who made sure all twelve of us children grew up in church. For it was there in a small country church that I met Jesus.

CONTENTS

INTRODUCTION

Where did life begin?
Did mankind evolve from some other life form?
Was there some massive explosion in the atmosphere, and all the pieces
randomly came together? If that is true, where did all the pieces come from?
Did mankind evolve?

I f you want to know the answers to these questions and more, this book was written for you. Our schools teach that evolution is how we came to be in this world, and there are several other theories of how life began, which I will cover in the first chapter. Science tells us that the earth has existed for billions of years, but it cannot tell us the origins of life. Furthermore, recorded history only goes back approximately 6,000 years. That time frame corresponds to the teachings of the Bible.

Regardless of what you may believe, there is no scientific way to prove any theory of how life began. In order to be scientifically verified, something has to be observed and reproduced in a laboratory. Men claim that they have cloned animals in the likeness of the original; however, the reproduction of another human has not been done. The beginning of human life cannot be observed, nor can it be reproduced in any laboratory. Therefore, science cannot tell us with any certainty where life began.

If you are like me, the thought of where we came from would be interesting to know. We should at least examine the information and not completely accept what we are told through our educational systems and multimedia sources. The Bible says in Proverbs 20:27 that the spirit of man searches all things, seeking to know the why and how of things. Have you ever thought about what sets mankind apart from all other life forms on Earth and why humans are so different? Science tells us man is just one step above monkeys, yet there is a vast difference in the life and environment of animals and man.

Educated man will tell you that if you believe the Bible, you have to have faith in what it states. Furthermore, they will label you as someone who is uneducated. The Bible is foolishness to mankind because it does require faith for you to believe it. If you have a solid foundation for what you believe to be true, what is the basis of that belief? If you are told something over and over again, do you then accept it as true? Do you ever check for the validity of what you are told, or does it matter? Evolution has become the accepted way in which life began, yet, when you research the matter, there are other theories for the origin of life.

Regardless of what you accept, you will believe by faith. By man's nature, he is led to believe in something; he is not forced to accept anything. The truthfulness of the matter is irrelevant. So then, when you believe something that is not proven to be fact, what is the basis of that belief—is it not faith, or is it man just picking and choosing what he wants to believe, whether factual or not?

I am very thankful for my education and the opportunities it gave me in life. However, Proverbs 1:7 says, "The fear of the Lord *is* the beginning of knowledge, *But* fools despise wisdom and instruction." America has thrown God out of our schools, and I feel that true knowledge no longer exists in our public education system. The beginning is the first step in attaining knowledge. Where do you go to get your true knowledge?

If you are open-minded enough to look at the different theories of life, whatever you choose to believe will require you to believe by faith, not science. Man claims to be knowledgeable, yet he drifts along, following an idea that is not proven. You will choose what you want to believe, and all mankind will follow in some way. Often, man will go down a path of life not knowing where he is going just because it requires some form of effort to change. However, throughout life you will make decisions that will affect the rest of your life, so it should matter whether or not it is true. The choices you make now will affect the decisions you will make for the rest of your life.

If you believe that life originated by evolution, there is something you need to know. If you put a single-cell organism in a lab and try to recreate it, you will get another single-cell organism. How, then, does something with one cell become a human body that has millions of cells? Consider all the multiple events that would have to happen over time for man to be as he is today—the different races, colors, and languages all over the world. There are many questions man should be asking about human life. The human body and mind are so complex that no one has the answer to those questions. Man does not have the answers, even though he claims he is knowledgeable. If the consensus is that nothing can be proved, will you believe something based upon what you are told, or are you willing to look for other answers? Whatever you choose to do, will it be by faith or science that leads you to your conclusions?

Through reading the Bible, I have found what I believe about God, creation, and mankind. If you are not aware of what the Bible says about creation and the character of man, know that God created all people with a purpose in life, and man was created to live forever, somewhere. You may say that you don't believe the Bible. In the depths of your heart and mind, does God exist? If God does not exist, there is nothing more to life than a vapor that appears for a short while and then disappears. If God does not exist, life has no meaning. But God does exist. Furthermore, the Bible tells us that God, Jesus Christ, the Holy Spirit, and the Bible are all "ONE." Therefore, you cannot say you believe in God but do not believe in Christ, the Holy Spirit, and the Bible. It is all or none; you cannot pick and choose what to believe. You cannot draw a line and separate one from the other.

I have used the Bible to formulate my beliefs. The Bible tells us the real story of mankind, who we are and when life started. There are many theories of when life began, and I will present a limited evaluation of some of those theories in these pages. The Bible, the world around me, and the behavior of all mankind tell me I was created in the image of God. To understand where I get the basis of my belief, you will need to get out your Bible and follow along because I will use almost all of it. I know that in some situations, I may take the scripture out of its implied meaning. Usually, when this happens, man is trying to justify his actions and behaviors. My intent is to show how holy and righteous God is and how sinful I am, as well as all mankind. I know who Jesus Christ is. He is my Savior and Lord. When you get out your Bible, also get out a mirror and take a good look at yourself. The Bible will tell you who you really are, not how you perceive yourself to be. Hopefully, through seeing what is written in the Bible, you will know that you were created in the image of God and come to know Jesus Christ as well.

I have used a lot of scripture verses in this book to reveal the true heart of man and the nature of God. My intent is not to do a Bible survey but for you to know what the Bible says, as there are many people and some Christians who do not know what is within the covers of the Holy Bible. It is very clear that man did not evolve. Man today would destroy every person who did not conform to his way of life. Something loving and good had to exist in this world for it to have existed as long as it has.

IN THE BEGINNING: MAN AND TIME

In the beginning God created the heavens and the earth.
—Genesis 1:1

When was the beginning?
Was it when heaven and earth were formed or when human life began?
Could creation have happened in six days, as the Bible describes?

There are many theories about where we came from and the formation of our universe. Every person may have his own opinion; however, I will look at some of the more prevalent theories and a few others you may not know about.

Before we get into the theories of life, let's see what is in a theory. A theory is systematic, organized knowledge applicable to a wide variety of circumstances. It is especially a system of assumptions accepted as principles, rules, and procedures devised to analyze, predict, and explain the nature or behavior of a specified set of phenomena. Such knowledge and systems are distinguished from experiment or practice. Other terms used are abstract reasoning, speculation, hypothesis, or supposition.[1] When you believe man's theories, you are using assumptions or speculations to analyze what

---

[1] "Theory," *The American Heritage Dictionary of the English Language.*

1

is considered true. Furthermore, the system of knowledge used cannot be proven. Therefore, you will choose what you want to believe.

EVOLUTION

The theory that we see and hear about the most is evolution, which is taught to our children in schools as fact when it cannot be proven as such. What is evolution and its concepts that make mankind want to accept it as fact? In *Mosby's Medical, Nursing and Allied Health Dictionary,* evolution is defined as a gradual, orderly, and continuous process of change and development from one state to another. It involves a progressive advancement from a simple to a more complex state through modification, differentiation, and growth. It tells of the origin and propagation of all plant and animal species, including humans. It further states all life develops from lower to higher forms through natural selection, mutation, and inbreeding. The *American Heritage Dictionary of the English Language* states there are significant, different, and more complex changes from the original. With all the violence and mass killings in our country today, are we progressing and developing to a higher form of life? The theory of evolution states changes "may" occur over time so that descendants will differ from their ancestors.

This theory may sound okay to the masses of people, but somewhere there had to be some kind of life form. Where did it come from? Furthermore, life, when put in a laboratory, does not change from simple forms to more complex ones. Also, inorganic matter does not turn into organic matter; rocks do not come to life. Nothing has changed in time; we are born, we grow from an infant to sometimes old age, and then we die. Does man think that as he grows, he is evolving? Where did man acquire morals, feelings, guilt and become responsible? Man seeks answers to life, but he often follows a path that has no basis in truth. He follows because everyone else believes it, or that is what he is told, and he accepts it as fact.

BIG BANG THEORY

The big bang theory states the whole universe evolved in a single moment. Everything fell into place after the explosion and has expanded ever since. We could ask, where did the energy come from for the explosion to take place? Furthermore, where did all the pieces come from that formed our universe? Also, would you not want to know what holds the universe together and keeps it functioning in an orderly manner? Events before the big bang are not defined because there is no way to measure what was before the explosion. Time began with the big bang.[2] There are many people who feel that life began after a big explosion. Does this philosophy have any basis in your beliefs? Whether it is reason, knowledge, or superstition, this theory is well-accepted by many people today.

NATURALISM

Naturalism is another theory some people believe today. You may be more familiar with the term "humanism." Naturalism conforms to nature and is defined as a factual or a realistic representation. It is a philosophy that all phenomena can be explained in terms of natural causes and laws. It cannot be attributed to moral, spiritual, or supernatural significance.[3] *Humanism* means the quality or condition of being human, but humanism is equated with "naturalism" in that it rejects all supernatural reasons for man's existence. It relies on reason, science, democracy, and compassion. According to the tenets of humanism, there is nothing supernatural about who you are. Your moral values are formed in human nature and experience alone. Humanism is a positive attitude about the world centered on human experience, thought, and hope. Honesty, integrity, truthfulness,

---

[2] John F. MacArthur, *The Battle for the Beginning: The Bible on Creation and the Fall of Adam* (Edinburgh, Scotland: Thomas Nelson, 2001).

[3] "Naturalism," *The American Heritage Dictionary of the English Language.*

and responsibility all have a rational basis to guide you in life.[4] But where can you find honesty, integrity, truthfulness, and responsibility in our world today? Furthermore, if your morals are formed by human nature, why should your conscience bother you in anything you do? If everything you do is positive, why do people have bad feelings? We all have a conscience. We know right from wrong, and bad feelings do affect how we live.

In the vein of naturalism, *natural selection* is the evolutionary process by which organisms adapt to their environment to survive and propagate the species, and those unfit are eliminated.[5] You have certain characteristics that give you an advantage for survival in your environment. This is another term for "survival of the fittest." If that is the way man has evolved, you would think that there would be some perfect people by now. Furthermore, people born today are of all colors, shapes, and sizes, and others are born with diseases and disabilities. If only certain types of people survive, this should not be happening unless we are still in a transition period of development, and it will happen sometime in the future.

COMMON DESCENT

The theory of common descent states that all organisms have a common ancestor. Charles Darwin proposed this theory by an evolutionary process, suggesting that all organisms had a common ancestor and that they diverged through random variations and struggled for existence. Similarly, universal common descent states all known forms of life are based on the same fundamental biochemical organization. The species living today are but a small part of those species that blind destiny has produced. Perhaps all living animals originated from one living filament.[6]

When words like "blind destiny" are used to justify a concept, it should

---

[4] "Definition of Humanism," *The American Humanist Association*, Accessed February 5, 2024, https://americanhumanist.org/what-is-humanism/definition-of-humanism/.
[5] "Natural selection," *Mosby's Medical, Nursing and Allied Health Dictionary*.
[6] "Universal Common Descent," *National Center for Science Education*, https://ncse.ngo/universal-common-descent.

tell you that it does not have a fundamental basis for you to believe. As I get older and see what is happening in the world today, I think people do not have a foundation in which they believe. They just go with the wind, whatever direction it blows. One thing that can be taken from the theory of universal common descent is that we are offsprings of our ancestors.

OTHER THEORIES

Even with the theories of evolution, the big bang, naturalism, and common descent, scientists continue to debate the origins of life. Some believe life began three billion years ago when an electric spark caused different molecules to become larger and larger, and life began. Life could have begun when molecules of life met on clay and, over time, organized themselves. There is also the possibility of a deep-sea vent, with life developing underwater. Another possibility is that ice covered the ocean at one time. The sun was not as bright, thereby allowing life to somehow begin under the ice. We do know that human life has RNA and DNA formations, but how did it get there? Could life have evolved with simple beginnings when smaller molecules interacted with each other and life began? Last of all, life may have come here from space. These theories use a lot of terms such as may, could, might and possibly telling us it is only speculation.[7]

Science does tell us that genetics (or heredity) is seen in all human life. Genetics is the science that studies hereditary traits or characteristics passed from parents to offspring.[8] Heredity is the process where traits and conditions are passed or transmitted from generation to generation, resulting in resemblances through descent from both parents. Those traits are both male and female. It is the sum of the qualities inherited from your ancestors, and those qualities can be transmitted into future human life.

Genetic characteristics can be proven and shown over a period of time.

---

[7] Charles Q. Choi, Scott Dutfield, "Seven Theories on the Origin of Life," *Live Science*, February 14, 2022, https://www.livescience.com/13363-7-theories-origin-life.html.

[8] "Genetics," *Mosby's Medical, Nursing and Allied Health Dictionary.*

The Bible says in Genesis 1:12, "And the earth brought forth grass, the herb that yields seed according to its kind, and the tree that yields fruit, whose seed is in itself according to its kind. And God saw that it was good."

CREATIONISM

According to the biblical account in Genesis, our descent has one source, and everything was created mature or as an adult. All plant and animal life, including humans, was created with the ability to multiply and replenish the earth, as stated in the Bible. Most scientists do not believe in the theory of creationism because of a lack of evidence, yet there are questions with any scientific theory about the origin of life. Does creationism bring doubts into your mind? Because there is no evidence, man, by his own nature, seeks answers from creation rather than looking at the Creator.

GOD IS ABOVE ALL CREATION

The Bible account of creation starts with God—who He is, where He came from, and how long He has existed. God's Word says in Isaiah 43:13, "Indeed before the day was, I am He; And there is no one who can deliver you out of My hand: I work, and who will reverse it?" *Before the day was* means He is self-sufficient and self-existent. In Hebrews 7:3, the Bible tells us that Jesus was without father, without mother, without genealogy, having neither beginning of days nor end of life, but made like the Son of God, and remains a priest continually. The Holy Trinity consists of God, Jesus Christ, and the Holy Spirit, which I will explain in more detail later in the book. The Bible tells us that God is not flesh and blood: "It is a difficult thing that the king requests, and there is no other who can tell it to the king except the gods, whose dwelling is not with flesh" (Daniel 2:11). By man's thinking, if God is not flesh, how can He exist? The Bible tells us very plainly that God is spirit, and the Spirit of God knows the spirit in man. In Exodus 33:23, God passes by Moses and tells him, "Then I will take away My hand, and you shall see My back; but My face shall not be seen." Moses spent forty days with God on top of Mt. Sinai and spoke with Him often but never saw His face.

God's throne is from everlasting. We read in Isaiah 57:15 that God inhabits eternity: "For thus says the High and Lofty One Who inhabits eternity, whose name is Holy: 'I dwell in the high and holy place, with him who has a contrite and humble spirit, to revive the spirit of the humble, and to revive the heart of the contrite ones.'" God's thoughts are eternal thoughts. How, then, do we explain God's existence or who He is? In Exodus 9:14, we read, "For at this time I will send all My plagues to your very heart, and on your servants and on your people, that you may know that there is none like Me in all the earth." There is no one to compare God with; there is none other. Jeremiah 23:24 says, "'Can anyone hide himself in secret places, so I shall not see him?' says the Lord. 'Do I not fill heaven and the earth?' says the Lord." God is everywhere at all times. Wherever we are and wherever we go, God will always be there. With man, it is sometimes said that things can be "out of sight, out of mind." The Bible says in Isaiah 40:28 that His understanding is unsearchable. In Romans 11:34, we read, "For who has known the mind of the Lord? Or who has become His counselor?" We do not know, and we don't have a reason to know why God does the things He does. Everything is naked and open to Him, and all things are done for His purposes and glory.

Regardless of what man tries to do or what he thinks he can do, man's inquiring mind will never know about God's plan or what to do about Him. As the heavens are higher than the earth, God's ways are higher than man's ways (Isaiah 55:9). Revelation 1:8 says God is "the Beginning and the End," and Exodus 3:14 states, "I AM WHO I AM," which tells us there is no past tense nor future tense with God. Later in Exodus 9:14, we read God's words, "that you may know that there is none like Me in all the earth." God cannot be compared to anyone else. Psalm 102:12 says, "But You, O LORD, shall endure forever, and the remembrance of Your name to all generations." God will always exist. There was no one before God, and there will not be anyone after Him.

CREATION IS SUBJECT TO GOD'S PLAN AND ORDER

Man will seek to find answers in the imaginations of his own heart because there is no one to turn to other than his own created gods. The Bible says in Isaiah 44:24, "Thus says the Lord your Redeemer and He who formed you from the womb: 'I am the Lord who makes all things, Who stretches out the heavens all alone, Who spreads abroad the earth by Myself.'" There was not anyone else who made anything. God is not subject to the laws of nature. With evolution, something had to happen for life to exist; there had to be something out there for matter or an organism to develop. With all other theories, life had to evolve from something; it could not evolve from nothing. With God, He spoke, and something was created from nothing. God did not have anything to use to make anything; He spoke, and it existed.

Hebrews 4:3 tells us God had a plan, and it was finished from the foundation of the world. God had a plan for all creation and how it was to be and function. The world was created by a being of infinite wisdom and power who was before time and before anything existed. Furthermore, the Bible tells us in 1 Corinthians 14:40 that all things of God are done decently and in order. How the world functions has order to it, but man has made it chaotic.

The Bible has more to tell us of God's creation. Job 26:7 says God "hangs the earth on nothing," and Isaiah 40:22 says that God sits above the circle of the earth. If scientists would have read the Bible long ago, they would have known the world is round and not flat! There was no blueprint except what was in the mind of God. He commanded creation, and it happened. The world as we know it did not come about by random events. Creation was specific to God's plan and order.

WHAT SETS MAN APART FROM ALL OTHER CREATION

The Bible says in Genesis chapter one that all creation took place in six days. There was total darkness, and the Spirit of God moved upon the face of the waters (1:2). The first day God created light and separated it from the darkness, calling light day and the darkness night (1:3–5). On the second day, God created heaven and earth (1:6–8). On the third day, God gathered the seas and dry lands together in their places, and the earth brought forth all manner of plant life (1:9–12). And all life had its seed within itself to reproduce a likeness of itself. On the fourth day, God created the sun, moon, and stars for signs, seasons, and for days and years (1:14–18). Before creation, there was no time; therefore, how can man say the world has existed for billions of years? God made two great lights, one to rule by day and the other to rule by night. And God set the sun, moon, and stars in the firmament of heaven. On the fifth day, God created all sea life and every winged fowl (1:20–22). God created great whales and every living creature in the seas. On the sixth day, God created all life that lived on the earth, including mankind (1:24–27). Everything that exists was created in six days, as described in Genesis 1.

God created all other living organisms before He created man. Mankind was last in His creation. In all of God's creation, He said, "Let there be light, let there be earth and seas, let there be vegetative life on earth, let there be stars in the universe and let there be life in the seas, sky and land." However, in verse 26, God said, "Let Us make man in Our image, according to Our likeness; let them have dominion over . . . all the earth." Here, we read that God is more than just Spirit. "Us" and "Our" are plural, revealing that God is not just one. God is three, and I will explain this in more detail later. The Bible says in Genesis 2:7, "And the LORD God formed man of the dust of the ground, and breathed into his nostrils the breath of life; and man became a living being." In all creation, God spoke, and it happened. However, when He created man, He took His time because man was made in the image and likeness of God. The Bible says in Job 33:4 that the breath of God is what gives man life. The breath of God is what sets man apart from all other life.

God breathed into man's nostrils, and he became a living soul. The Bible states man has a soul (Genesis 2:7 KJV). Furthermore, it does not say anywhere in the Bible that other life forms have a soul. *The American*

9

Heritage Dictionary of the English Language defines a soul as the being separate from the body and involves your feelings, thinking, actions, and morals. This includes your conscience, which knows right from wrong. Man has an internalized set of values and standards that God put inside us; all mankind knows God.

Psalm 119:73 says that God's hands made and fashioned us. Identity and sexuality are issues in the world we live in today, but Genesis 1:27 says God created all mankind, male and female. I know there are people born with physical, developmental, and other forms of abnormalities that may make them look different. However, if someone is human, the Bible states they are male or female. God is the one and only designer and maker of all mankind. In most all forms of life, God created male and female to replenish the earth as the Bible instructs. With creation, the genetic traits were put there from the beginning; they did not evolve over billions of years.

OUR QUEST FOR UNDERSTANDING

Man cannot explain God other than what is written in the Bible. Then, what is man to do to find the answers? The Bible tells us in Ecclesiastes 8:17, "Then I saw all the work of God, that a man cannot find out the work that is done under the sun. For though a man labors to discover it, yet he will not find it; moreover, though a wise man attempts to know it, he will not be able to find it." Man will always attempt to find answers to life and where we came from. However, man will never know the mind of God.

Ecclesiastes 3:11 says that God "has made everything beautiful in its time. Also, He has put eternity in their hearts, except that no one can find out the work that God does from the beginning to end." Mankind will never find the answer in his own knowledge and wisdom. Man does not know, and he never will know. But if man will seek God, then God will reveal to him what he needs to know. The first step is knowing God.

QUESTIONS FOR REFLECTION

1. What theories for the origin of life have shaped your view of how the universe began?

2. Do you struggle with reconciling theoretical science with the creation account in the Word of God?

3. How can the idea that all theories, both religious and scientific, require faith and belief help you resolve any doubts about the veracity of God's Word regarding the creation account?

FOR I AM FEARFULLY AND WONDERFULLY MADE: GOD'S DESIGN

I am the Lord, who makes all things.
—ISAIAH 44:24

When God created everything except mankind, He said His creation was good (Genesis 1:1–25). But when God created man and saw all the creation together, He said it was *very* good (Genesis 1:31). The creation of man last reveals that mankind was not involved in any part of creation. Creation was totally of God. Furthermore, the creation of man reflects the honor God put on him; however, it showed man he had nothing to do with any of it. Everything man needed in life was before his eyes. He didn't have to do anything to please God other than obey Him. When God said, "Let Us make man in Our image, after Our likeness" (1:26), we see God's love and affection. God's plan and purpose demonstrated that man had a higher favor in His creation. In Genesis 2:7, we read, "And the Lord God formed man of the dust of the ground, and breathed into his nostrils the breath of life; and man became a living being." That part of man came from God, not our earthly parents.

The soul of man can be described in many ways. The *Pictorial Bible Dictionary* states the soul is the non-material ego of man in its ordinary relationships with the earth and physical things. The soul functions in different ways. It consists of the mind, which is the self in its rational functions, and the heart, which manifests itself in our attitudes and emotions. The will is the self-choosing and deciding part of the soul. The different functional parts of the soul often overlap one another. You may feel that other life forms on Earth have some of these qualities. However, only man was created in the image and likeness of God.

BODY, SOUL, AND SPIRIT

Man is made of three distinct entities: his body, soul, and spirit. His body will return to the dust from which it came someday. His soul and spirit will spend eternity somewhere else. Modern non-Christian psychology ignores or denies the existence of the soul. It claims the self is a behavior pattern, that a person has an awareness of his world without having a conscience. However, his conscience guides him in the decisions he will make. In Proverbs 20:27, the Bible says, "The spirit of man is the lamp of the Lord, searching all the inner depths of his heart." Man's soul has a light from God, and his conscience reveals what is right and wrong.

THE HUMAN SOUL

What do you know about your soul? Is it the part of you that seeks to find a partner in life that shares in your beliefs and values? The Bible tells us the soul is much more than that. In Isaiah 57:16, the Bible says that God made man's soul. In Ezekiel 18:4, we read that all souls belong to God. The Bible also says your soul knows things and has feelings. In Psalm 42:6, for example, we read that our souls can become depressed and in Psalm 143:6, our souls long for God like a thirsty land. 1 Peter 2:11 says our flesh and soul war against each other. They war because our flesh has a sin nature and our soul is from God.

In Proverbs 8:36, we read that whoever sins against God wrongs his own soul, and Ezekiel 18:20 says, "The soul who sins shall die. The son shall not bear the guilt of the father, nor the father bear the guilt of the son. The righteousness of the righteous shall be upon himself, and the wickedness of the wicked shall be on himself." Our soul is a part of everything we are.

Jesus says in Matthew 16:26, "For what profit is it to a man if he gains the whole world, and loses his own soul? Or what will a man give in exchange for his soul?" Are you storing up riches for your life here on earth? In Isaiah 57:16, we read that God will not contend for our souls forever. God knows when we reach a point in our lives when we will never seek Him again. Does that create any fear in you? Your soul will spend eternity somewhere.

THE HUMAN SPIRIT

What about mankind's spirit? Do we have a spirit that dwells in our souls? In Zechariah 12:1, we read that God formed our spirits, and in Psalm 104:30 that God sent forth His Spirit when man was created. James 2:26 says the body without the spirit is dead. The spirit in man is from God and connects him back to God. In Ecclesiastes 8:8, we read that mankind does not have power over his own spirit. In Isaiah 26:9, the Bible says the spirit in man seeks God. Job 32:8 says, "But there is a spirit in man, and the breath of the Almighty gives him understanding." In Isaiah 11:2, we see that we get knowledge, wisdom, counsel, fear of the Lord, and power from our spirit. In Isaiah 38:16, we see there is life in the spirit because it is from God. Life did not come through evolution; it came through someone who lives.

THE HUMAN BODY

In 1 Corinthians 15:44, we read, "There is a natural body, and there is a spiritual body." There is more to our bodies than just flesh and blood! We have a soul and spirit that helps us to know and understand the world in which we live. Ecclesiastes 12:7 tells us the dust (our bodies) will return to the earth as it was, and the spirit will return to God who gave it. That part within us that reveals our Creator will return to God when we die. I have heard it said that our soul and spirit will both spend eternity in hell if we do not accept Christ as our Savior. Based upon the scriptures, I do feel that our soul and spirit are two different entities God has put in all mankind. In Hebrews 4:12, we read that "the word of God is living and powerful, and sharper than any two-edged sword, piercing even to the division of soul and spirit, and of joints and marrow, and is a discerner of the thoughts and intents of the heart." The Word of God can separate our soul from the spirit. Real life is within the soul and spirit of every person. It is not in the physical body of mortal man, which came through our ancestors.

In all these verses, we see clearly that God gave man a soul and spirit. It is how he interacts with God, mankind, and the world in which he lives. Hebrews 6:19 says that hope is the anchor of the soul, which is sure and steadfast.

Any hope you have in life did not evolve—it came from your soul. Do you have hope for the future? The Bible says in James 1:21 to lay aside all filthiness and sin and receive with meekness the implanted word, which is able to save your soul. Your soul will live forever somewhere, and you get to decide where.

We do not know much about the human body. Furthermore, man knows very little about his soul, which God put within each of us when we were conceived. The Bible says in Matthew 19:4, "Have you not read that He who made them at the beginning made them male and female." Man thinks he can alter what God has created. We may be able to medically and surgically change the outward appearance of our sex, but there is nothing we can do to change our soul and spirit.

Even though man was created in God's image, we do not have God's nature. God does not have a physical body, but man has a living soul that does bear God's likeness. "Then God blessed them and God said to them, 'Be fruitful and multiply; fill the earth and subdue it; have dominion over the fish of the sea, over the birds of the air, and over every living thing that moves on the earth'" (Genesis 1:28). God put man in charge over every living thing that existed on earth. Man had nothing to do with any of God's creation, yet he is given control over all of it.

Then, what is man that God is mindful of him? When we consider the heavens, sun, moon, stars, and all of God's creation, why did He give so much favor to man (Psalm 8:3–4)? When you look at all God has created, why did God put so much of Himself into mankind? If we evolved, man is of no more importance than anything else that exists on earth. Furthermore, if we evolved, there is no design or purpose in who we are. We are just objects that adapted to our environment. In God's picture, man is His crowning creation. In Psalm 8:5 the psalmist states, God crowned man with glory and honor.

THE SANCTITY OF LIFE

Every person is either male or female, and each of us is a living soul. Do you want to know more about yourself? The Bible says in Jeremiah 1:5, "Before I formed you in the womb I knew you." Job 31:15 says, "Did not He who made me in the womb make them? Did not the same One fashion us in the womb?" Psalm 139:15 reads, "My frame was not hidden from You, when I was made in secret, and skillfully wrought in the lowest parts of the earth."

When I was much younger and did not know what the Bible said, I was sympathetic to a woman possibly having an abortion in extreme circumstances. However, since coming to know what the Bible says about life, abortion is just another choice man has made to disobey God. When we read God's Word, which is given to man to guide and direct him in life, we will find He was there when we were conceived. It should tell us just how precious life is to God. I believe if there is conception, then God has a plan and purpose for your life. Regardless of the situation—whether rape, incest, violence, or between husband and wife—if there is conception, it was God's plan. All life is from God, and it is special. Maybe in your parents' eyes, you came forth by accident, but it was planned by God.

He was there before you and I were conceived. That is how precious and important you are to God! But God is not always important to man. Man wants a plan that fits into his lifestyle in the world in which he lives today.

Throughout the Bible, man has chosen to disobey God. Aborting or sacrificing a baby for one's own gain is nothing new to mankind. The Bible tells us in 2 Kings 23:10 that people sacrificed their children by making them walk through fire to their god, Molech. We read in Amos 5:26 that Chiun was an idol man made for himself. Mankind has made himself his own god. Self-gratification is what is most important in our world today.

Man does not realize if God is there before we are conceived, then He is everywhere we are. The Bible tells us in Psalm 139 that God knows everything about us. In verse 3, we read: "You are acquainted with all my ways." In verse 7 it says, "Where can I go from Your Spirit? Or where can I flee from Your presence?" In verse 12, we find we cannot hide in the dark because darkness and light are the same to Him. And verse 14 says, "I am fearfully and wonderfully made; marvelous are Your works, and that my soul knows very well."

The Bible tells us that man knows he was created by God. Furthermore, he knows he did not evolve from nothing. In Psalm 33:15, we read that God fashioned the hearts of man individually. We should be astonished at how the human body functions. It all works together in harmony as God planned! Ephesians 2:10 reads that "we are His workmanship, created in Christ Jesus for good works." It was God who created us.

Most people just exist with little knowledge of God or His purposes. The Bible says in Isaiah 43:7, "Everyone who is called by My name, whom I have created for my glory; I have formed him, yes, I have made him." We were formed for God's glory and purpose. We will never fully understand God because His ways are higher than ours. If we seek Him with all our hearts, we can know Him and know His plan for our lives. Even though God is Spirit, we can reach out to Him through Jesus Christ. By receiving Jesus Christ, we can know God.

The Body with Physical Limitations

If you are observant of the world around you, there will be people who have disabilities, which may cause you to ask why someone is born differently. There are many people with disabilities, whether through birth defects, hereditary diseases, man's bad habits, accidents, or injury. Furthermore, there are people born having a greater mix of male or female hormones yet having physical characteristics of the opposite sex. There are others who experience struggles with sexual identity, even though the Bible is very plain in saying we are either male or female. When you encounter people with birth defects or acquired disabilities, you may ask why did this happen or why God allowed it? If we have a loving God, why is it that there are people with disabilities? Probably all of us know someone who has some type of physical or mental impairment. If we are created in the image of God, why do bad things happen to people?

I have personally met and talked with two people who have different types of physical disabilities. The first is David Ring, who was born with cerebral palsy. From his book *The Boy Born Dead*, he was pronounced dead shortly after he was born. He was placed on a table in the corner of the delivery room and declared dead. His mother saw some movement in him, and he began to fight to live. He miraculously survived. He faced so many odds to live, and by the time he was fifteen, he was an orphan. He was placed with various relatives and in foster homes. He had problems walking and communicating with people when talking. Just living day-to-day was a tremendous challenge. During that very difficult time in his life, he came to know a family who led him to Jesus Christ. Today, he is internationally known as an evangelist and tells everyone how God cared for him when it seemed no one else did. He tells everyone, "God does not throw away broken things; God uses broken things." I think he would tell you that real life is not in a broken body; real life is knowing you are in the hands of God our Creator.[9]

---

[9] David Ring, et all, *The Boy Born Dead* (Michigan, US: Baker Books, 2016), 238.

Another person I have met and talked with is Tim Lee. Tim was almost twenty-one years old and in the US Marines during the Vietnam War. He stepped on a box land mine and lost both of his legs almost instantly. He had less than two weeks remaining in his tour of duty. He would have come home in good health, yet in the twinkling of an eye, his life forever changed. In his book, *Born on the Fifth of July*, he says, "Had I not taken that step, had my foot not triggered a land mine, would I have become an evangelist? Would my story resonate with thousands who have heard my testimony? How many people who have made decisions to ask Christ into their lives would not have done so had I kept my legs?"[10] God used his personal tragedy for His glory. Today, Tim Lee of Tim Lee Ministries preaches all over this country and in many places across the world. I believe if you talked with Tim Lee today, he would say he suffered a lot with multiple surgeries since losing his legs, but because of this tragedy, he found his life in God, his Creator.

I have personally met these two men, read their books, and heard their testimonies. I know there are many other people who have found there are no disabilities or limitations with God our Creator. Some people are born with physical and mental limitations; however, many people choose to limit God. His Word says He would open the windows of heaven to us *if* we would put Him first in our lives. We will encounter people with disabilities every day of our lives and wonder, "Why?" But another question we should consider even more is why we usually feel uncomfortable around these people. Why are some people bullied, even small children? Do we judge others when the Bible clearly says God is the only true judge? We see a shadow of a person and judge them when God sees their heart. Are we prejudiced in feeling that we are better than those around us? Christians, too often, can be just as judgmental as others in how they look at people who are different.

---

[10] Tim Lee, et al, *Born on the Fifth of July* (AE Academic Publishing, 2018), 214–215.

UNIQUELY CREATED FOR HIS GLORY

God made each of us unique; there is no one else like you or me. Isaiah 43:21 says, "This people I have formed for Myself; they shall declare My praise." Regardless of our disabilities, limitations, or how different we may be, we were made for God's glory. I have heard people ask, "Why did an innocent person die in an accident and the person who caused the accident live?" We do not know why, and we will never understand God's purpose. Furthermore, God does not force His plan on us. Even though we are made for God's glory, every person gets to choose what he wants to do with his life.

Most Christians know that mankind's sin nature is part of the reason we have more physical problems in life now. In John 9:1–3, we read the disciples came to Christ and asked Him of the blind man, "Rabbi, who sinned, this man or his parents, that he was born blind?" Jesus answers them by saying, "Neither this man nor his parents sinned, but that the works of God should be revealed in him." Not everyone is born normal, the word we use to describe people. I once heard a doctor say, "Normal is a place in Illinois; it is not a word to describe anyone." Normal is an expression mankind uses to categorize groups of people when, in reality, normal is very subjective. God did not create everyone "normal." We read in Jeremiah 2:21 that God planted man from a noble vine, a seed of the highest quality. In 1 Corinthians 15:38 we read that God gives a body as He pleases, and to each seed its own body. You would think that if every human had the seed of God, everyone would have a perfect body. But man is in the physical lineage of Adam, who sinned. Man can only be perfect in Jesus Christ through faith, not through the flesh.

What about man and his body? In 1 Timothy 4:4, we read that every creature of God is good. In 1 Corinthians chapter 12, Paul is talking about the body of the Church. However, the body of man could be stated just as well. In verse 24 it says God composed the body together. God created all people with different gifts and talents. We are all different, but we have the same Lord (12:5). Each person does things differently, but the same God works in all of us (12:6). Everyone has a different role, but the same Spirit works in every person (12:10–11). The body is one and has many parts, but functions as one (12:12) and is not one member, but many (12:14). No one part is better than another, nor is one part less useful than another (12:15–16). Do we look at people who are created in the image of God and judge them because they are different? Verse 17 asks if every part was the same, how would the body function? If we evolved, would we not be more alike? Yet we are so different. What would the world be like if we were all alike? In verse 18 we see God has put the body together as it has pleased Him. He has formed each part, each person, differently for His purpose. The body is many parts, yet one body (12:20). This world and our body do not function as a bunch of loose parts that somehow come together randomly in time. We find, rather, that every part of the body is important (12:21). Those parts that seem more feeble or insignificant are just as important. People who are different or disabled are necessary in God's creation. In fact, for the parts of the body that do not seem needed, God has given more honor, and with our unpresentable parts, we show greater modesty (12:23). Has God given more honor to these people because society looks at them differently?

In verse 25, we read there should not be any divisions in the body. Whether we be Jews, Gentiles, enslaved or free, regardless of color, race, nationality, culture, whole, disabled or different, we are all made to drink of the same one Spirit (12:13). Mankind has very limited knowledge of his body. Furthermore, he cannot see what is in the heart of the people he is around. We make opinions and sometimes judge people based on the limited time we are around them.

In 1 Samuel 16:7, God tells the prophet Samuel, "Do not look at his appearance or at his physical stature, because I have refused him. For the LORD does not see as man sees; for man looks at the outward appearance, but the LORD looks at the heart." We all have the same God who formed us. God has given us a body as it has pleased Him. In James 3:9, the Bible asks us: do we bless God and curse man who was made in the likeness of

God? We know people are different, and we see them all around us. When we see other people, we should remember that the God who created us is the same God who created them. We, too, should be looking at God the Creator rather than creation.

Those who are different or disabled can only become whole by magnifying and glorifying God. Do they trust, believe, and lean on God more than "normal" people? Are we who have the advantage of life in the physical world disabled in the spiritual world? Do we lean on ourselves more than God?

Suffering often brings people closer to God, often allowing God to use that person more. In Isaiah 14:24, we read, "Surely, as I have thought, so it shall come to pass, and as I have purposed, so it shall stand." In God's infinite wisdom and plan, He placed the right person in the right place to accomplish His purposes. Differences and disabilities are not limitations in the hands of God, the Creator. Mankind chooses to limit God because we look at our situation and not the strength of God. Jesus told His disciples, "Neither this man sinned nor his parents, but that the works of God should be made manifested in him."

We did not evolve. Rather, it was God who thoughtfully, wonderfully created each one of us in His image, according to His plan and purposes, so that His glory would be manifested in us.

QUESTIONS FOR REFLECTION

1. Psalms 139:14 says we are fearfully and wonderfully made; how do you think the body would function if it was not by design?
2. Evolution states we are continually evolving to a higher state; why are diseases still prevalent in our world today?

FROM IMMORTALITY TO DEATH: SIN'S COST

But each one is tempted when he is drawn away by his own desires and enticed. Then, when desire has conceived, it gives birth to sin; and sin, when it is full-grown, brings forth death.

—JAMES 1:14–15

If man was created in the image of God, why did he become so different from what God intended? In 2 Timothy 1:7, we read that God gave man a sound mind. The Bible says in Ecclesiastes 7:29, "Truly, this only I have found: that God made man upright, but they have sought out many ways to live." Jeremiah 2:21 tells us man was planted on a good vine with high-quality seed, yet he has turned into a degenerate plant of an alien vine. In Psalm 51:5, we read, "I was brought forth in iniquity." Even though we have a heavenly Father, we are brought into this world physically by our earthly mother and father. Since Adam, all mankind has been conceived with a sin nature.

God created man with a free will to choose what he wants and how he wants to live. Even though man was created for God's glory, God lets each person decide how he wants to live and gives man instructions on how to do so fruitfully. Adam and Eve chose to follow the route of disobedience and sin. They could have lived forever with God in the Garden of Eden, but disobedience took them to their death. They died, and so will all mankind who choose to follow that same path. Two trees stood in the Garden of Eden, the Tree of Life and the tree of the knowledge of good and evil. The Tree of Life did not appeal to them, but the other tree did. God explicitly told Adam in Genesis 2:17, "For in the day that you eat of it you shall surely die." Disobedience to God had consequences—their lives.

DISOBEDIENCE

What happened to man after being gloriously formed until his fall? Adam was created in the first chapter of Genesis to live forever, yet he fell from immortality to death in the third chapter of the Bible. How could man, God's crowning glory, start in Paradise and fall so far in such a short period of time? We see a similar fall in Exodus 15:24 when the Jewish people complained against Moses after crossing the Red Sea on dry ground. The people had been delivered out of bondage and set free, yet so quickly complained about their circumstances. Man does not see God when life is good, but he wants to know where He is when things go bad.

Do you dare look in the Bible and see what is in man's heart and soul? We can see some of the problems from the Bible, but only God knows the depths of man's heart. Man can only read the Scriptures and gather conclusions based upon what they say. All mankind is made of two opposing natures. We are in the lineage of Adam, who disobeyed God and sinned. The Bible tells us that sin, when it is finished, brings forth death (James 1:15). However, mankind was created in the image and likeness of God. In Colossians 3:10 and Ephesians 4:24, we read that the image of God consists in part of knowledge, righteousness, and holiness. Even though we are in the likeness of God, there is an infinite distance between God and man. Jesus Christ is the only exact image of God. Christ has the same nature as God because He *is* God. Man is a shadow of God's image; you see part of the character of the original. We have the soul and the spirit of God, but the body and flesh are of man.

When we think of God's image, we must realize that God is Spirit. He is not flesh, and there is no body. The soul bears God's likeness.

Knowledge, understanding, the will, and active power are attributes of the soul. They help man to know God and the world in which man lives. Jesus Christ did have a physical body, and mankind will probably have a body much like His in eternity.

When we look further at man beyond his heritage of two worlds, we see the role God had for man. There was a purpose: He was to have dominion over all of God's creation. God gave man the responsibility of caring for the Garden of Eden. God provided Adam with all he needed to sustain life. The trees and herbs of the Garden provided food for him, and he had a home in which to live. He did not have to do anything other than care for the Garden and obey God.

God saw that all life was created, male and female, to procreate and replenish the earth. All living things had that ability except man. God saw that man was alone and needed a helpmate to make him more complete. God knew man's needs and created for Adam the perfect partner. This was God's plan, His design for mankind to multiply and replenish the earth. When God created Eve, He created the helpmate Adam needed. Eve was formed by God, just as He formed Adam. God made one male for one female, one blood and one heritage. God ordained marriage and the family.

Creation came about because God spoke, and it happened. Adam knew that his existence came from God. God gave man His laws for us to live by, "Obey and live, disobey and die." God gave Adam explicit directions as to how he was to live in the Garden. Adam knew he was not to eat of the forbidden tree. What happened that he disobeyed God? We, like Adam, have decisions to make every day, and there are consequences to disobedience. With God, it is sin and death.

God told Adam what would happen, and the Bible warns all mankind of the consequences of sin. The Spirit of God is willing in man, but the flesh is weak (Mark 14:38). Even though the spirit is strong, most people allow the flesh to rule in their lives. Mankind's lusts, sensual desires, curious instincts, and Satan's lies and deception cause him to doubt God and His commandments. The Bible says in James 1:14–15, "Each one is tempted when he is drawn away by his own desires and enticed. Then, when desire has conceived, it gives birth to sin; and sin, when it is full-grown, brings forth death." In 2 Timothy 2:26, we read the devil is a snare who takes man captive at Satan's will. The Bible says all mankind will die someday because of our sin nature. We all have a choice, a decision to make and a life to gain.

Although God provided everything Adam needed in the Garden, man wanted more. We read in Genesis 3:1 that the serpent was more cunning than any beast of the Garden God had made. In Revelation 12:9, we see the serpent, called the Devil and Satan, were all the same. In Genesis 3:14, God told the serpent, "You are cursed more than all cattle, and more than every beast of the field; on your belly you shall go, and you shall eat dust all the days of your life."

Man is most vulnerable to fall into sin when alone, downcast, or when he sees something that appeals to the eye and the flesh. In Deuteronomy 9:16, we read man can change quickly. The serpent drew Eve away from Adam and God's presence; however, we are never out of the sight of God. The serpent told Eve she would not die if she ate of the tree of the knowledge of good and evil. Furthermore, he told her, "You will be like God, knowing good and evil" (Genesis 3:5). She took of the tree and then gave it to her husband, and he did eat (Genesis 3:6). Temptation often comes to man so subtly that he is deceived thinking he can handle it. Usually, by then, it already has its hold on him, and he tries to justify his actions. John 8:44 says the devil is a liar, and he was a murderer from the beginning.

Satan further deceives man about God's laws and commandments to cause him to question what God has said in the Bible. Satan changes the truth of God's Word into something that appeals to man's desires. Galatians 1:6 says man can turn away soon from the gospel of Christ, and 1 John 2:16 says, "For all that is in the world—the lust of the flesh, the lusts of the eyes and the pride of life—is not of the Father but is of the world." We all tend toward questioning God and seeking our own desires, as Philippians 2:21 says: "All men seek their own, not the things which are of Christ Jesus."

After eating of the tree of the knowledge of good and evil, Adam and

Eve's eyes were opened. Their souls revealed to them that they had sinned, and they were naked. Before there was sin, their conscience was clean. After they disobeyed God, they felt dirty. Before, there was no shame and guilt, just the innocence of being with God in Paradise. When mankind "knows" he has sinned, he has a guilty conscience. In James 1:13, we read, "Let no one say when he is tempted, 'I am tempted by God'; for God cannot be tempted by evil, nor does He Himself tempt anyone." Sin came from within man's heart. Sin is progressive—we covet or lust for something, and it festers in our hearts. When the sin is finished, we feel guilty. Those ill feelings affect everything we do.

Sin is the transgression of the law (1 John 3:4). Satan tries to make us discontent with our situation and the ambition to change it. Man wants his sensual desires to be gratified now, even though his actions go against God's commandments. The desires of the eyes and flesh appeal to mankind, even when God's Word tells us it will harm us rather than make us better. Then, man will often try to hide from God or blame others instead of taking responsibility for his sins: "It was not my fault."

Man's fall took place quickly in the Bible. Instead of seeing God's goodness in providing everything, man saw that God was holding something back from him. Man felt that the forbidden tree was all he needed to make him better and wise, yet it did neither. With their disobedience, Adam and Eve were driven out of the Garden of Eden so they could no longer eat from the Tree of Life. In Genesis 3:19, God told them, "For out of [the ground] you were taken; for dust you are, and to dust you shall return." God had told Adam he would die if he ate of that tree, and God was faithful and true to keep what He said.

PROSPERITY, FULLNESS OF BREAD

Another question could be asked regarding man's fall. God blessed man by giving him all he needed. Man was God's crowning glory in creation. Adam lived in a home, a Paradise in which he did nothing to prepare or attain. There are explicit warnings in the Bible to men who have much and feel they no longer need God. Could Adam have had any of those feelings? Ezekiel 16:49 tells us about the iniquity of man when he is full of bread and becomes prideful. In Deuteronomy 6:10–12, we read, "So shall it be, when the LORD your God brings you into the land of which He swore to your fathers, to Abraham, Isaac, and Jacob, to give you large and beautiful cities which you did not build, houses full of all good things, which you did not fill, hewn-out wells which you did not dig, vineyards and olive trees which you did not plant—when you have eaten and are full—then beware, lest you forget the LORD who brought you out of the land of Egypt, from the house of bondage." We need to be cautious about forgetting God in the day of plenty and prosperity. God had brought the Jewish people out of slavery into a good land. The people would no longer travel day-to-day and live in tents in a barren land. They would live in cities and have houses well furnished with gardens and well-watered lands. Proverbs 1:32 says that the complacency of fools will destroy them. They became proud of the security and sensual delights of the land. They exalted themselves with what they had done, never thinking about what God had provided. Proverbs 30:9 says that when we are full, we ask, "Who is the LORD?" Prosperity makes us proud of ourselves and forgetful of God. We feel we don't need Him anymore.

We see further in Hosea 13:6 that they were filled and their hearts were exalted, forgetting about the Lord. God took care of His people in the wilderness in a dry, barren land. He provided food and water when it could not be found for so great a multitude of people. Some of the people were unworthy and murmured against Moses and God for the sustenance they received. God directed the people to Canaan, the Promised Land. When they got there, they filled themselves full of the rich bounty of the land. The luxury and sensuality they found made them proud and secure. They began to think they had no further need of God. Their hearts were exalted and full of themselves; there was no room for God, who had given them everything. Jesus said in Luke 6:25, "Woe to you who are full, for you shall hunger." The world envies prosperous people. People who are wealthy see the world with a smile on their faces because they think they have nothing to worry about in life. They want to take it easy and live life to the fullest. Prosperity is not a concern for them other than maintaining their social standing in their community. With increased wealth, God becomes smaller and smaller in their hearts. Jesus warns us that people who are full shall one day hunger.

Jesus asks in Mark 8:37, "What will a man give in exchange for his soul?" In Revelation 3:17, we read, "Because you say, 'I am rich, have become wealthy, and have need of nothing'—and do not know that you are wretched, miserable, poor, blind, and naked." Those who are prosperous are often high minded of themselves and are delusional of their wealth. Their soul is starving when the body is full. Man looks at his body, while God is more interested in his heart and soul.

Adam and Eve had everything given to them, a Paradise in which to live and all manner of food needed to sustain life. They had God with them, who would make sure any other need was met. They had a secure place to live and had nothing to fear. We might ask: What more could man want? Because they sinned, we know Adam and Eve wanted more than what God provided. Was prosperity an issue in man's fall, or was his fall just an act of disobedience?

Deuteronomy 28:1–44 outlines the blessings man will receive for obedience versus the cursed life he will have for disobedience. In Exodus 19:5, God promises that if man will "obey my voice and keep My covenant, then [he] shall be a special treasure to Me above all people." What does obeying the law mean to you? The Bible tells us in 1 Samuel 15:22 that our offerings and sacrifices to God are not meaningful to Him if we are not obedient to His commandments. Obedience requires a heart determined to please God in all that we do.

What happened to man that caused him to become disobedient? In Ephesians 5:6, we read that man is easily deceived with empty words, which leads to the wrath of God. Adam and Eve listened to the lies and vain words of Satan and quickly turned their hearts from the truth. Deception comes about fast when we do not know what is true. There are consequences for disobedience; sin creates a barrier between man and God. Christians, too, lose their fellowship with God when they sin. When we choose to live the way we want, we will be disappointed in what we get.

Obedience or disobedience are choices each of us will make. We will make those decisions alone. No one will choose for us; it is something we will do in our hearts and souls. The Bible says in Deuteronomy 11:26–28, "Behold, I set before you today a blessing and a curse: the blessing, if you obey the commandments of the LORD your God which I command you today; and the curse, if you do not obey the commandments of the LORD your God." The decision is that simple. God said we will either be blessed or cursed. In 1 Samuel 12:15, the Bible says if we rebel against God's commandments, the hand of the Lord will be against us.

Jesus sums up the whole matter of obedience in Matthew 7:21: "Not everyone who says to Me, 'Lord, Lord,' shall enter into the kingdom of heaven, but he who does the will of My Father in heaven." Our outward appearance of following Christ will not be sufficient to get us to heaven. Words are not always indicators of what is true in man's heart. We may be deceiving our hearts into thinking we are obedient; however, God knows our hearts. Adam disobeyed God. Because of his sin, he was driven away from his Paradise home and died later. But God's plan for sin and death did not end with Adam. He had a plan to redeem man from the penalty of sin.

QUESTIONS FOR REFLECTION

1. Mark 14:38 says that the spirit is willing, but the flesh is weak. Where do you experience this tension most in your walk as a believer?

2. Is there something in your life that you are coveting, like Adam and Eve, not finding contentment in God's provision? How can you transform your mindset to see the goodness of God in your current situation?

3. How has fullness in one area of your life (finances, relationships, etc.) led to you feeling that you need God less?

4. Do you obey the laws of man? What is the consequence of disobeying those laws?

5. When things are going well in your life, do you ever think about God or only about your accomplishments?

BEFORE THE FOUNDATIONS OF THE WORLD: THERE WAS A PLAN

The heavens declare the glory of God;
and the firmament shows His handiwork.
—PSALM 19:1

What does "before the foundations of the world" mean to you? We see everything around us without thinking about how it came to be. If we look at any one part of life, we can only be amazed at the beauty of what exists. What we see around us did not come about by random pieces falling into their places. The greatest minds in all the world will never understand why there is order in the world and universe. There is a master designer who created all that we see. That master designer, God, said, "Let Us make man in Our image, according to Our likeness" (Genesis 1:26).

God is all-knowing, and He knew man would sin. Not only does God know the heart of all mankind, but He knows our thoughts as well as the intent of the heart. Nothing man does catches God by surprise. He knew Adam and Eve would sin, and He knows every person will also sin. From the beginning, it was God who reached down to mankind because man does not seek God of his own heart. It is the God-given spirit in man that will seek Him. Mankind, by his own sinful nature, does not want God.

But man is God's crowning glory of all His creation. What is man that God, Jesus Christ, and the Holy Spirit specifically formed him to be in the image and likeness of God? The Bible tells us that mankind, of all His creation, is the object of His plans and purposes. Everything that exists was purposed by God; it did not happen by chance. In Isaiah 46:11, the Bible says, "I have spoken it; I will also bring it to pass. I have purposed it; I will also do it." Isaiah 14:27 tells us what God purposes will stand for all time, and no one is able to turn back His hand. What, then, does God have planned for you and me? Do you want to know?

WHOSOEVER

In 2 Peter 3:9, we read that it is God's will that none should perish but that every person would come to repentance. John 3:16 says, "For God so loved the world that He gave His only begotten Son, that whosoever believes in Him should not perish but have everlasting life." It is God's plan that all mankind would come to Christ, be born again, and inherit a paradise home prepared by Him. Nicodemus, a ruler of the Jews in the time of Christ, came to Him, knowing that Jesus was of God. Jesus told him in John 3:3, "Most assuredly, I say to you, unless one is born again, he cannot see the kingdom of God." Nicodemus asked how he could go back into his mother's womb and be born again, and Jesus told him he had to be born of the Spirit of God to see His kingdom.

When God put the soul and spirit in all mankind, He said, "Whosoever believes in Me." Having godly parents and friends will not transcend through your flesh and cause you to be born again. Each of us, alone, will choose where we will spend eternity. In Titus 1:2, we read that eternal life for every person was promised by God before time began. God, in His foreknowledge, had a plan for man to escape the penalty of sin. In Matthew 25:34, we see that those born again have an inheritance prepared by God. From the beginning, man has had a choice to make about where he would spend eternity.

There was a plan for Adam and Eve, and there is a plan for all mankind who sin and disobey God. Romans 3:23 says, "For all have sinned and fall short of the glory of God." The question is not about man's sin but what he does when he sins. Jesus Christ came to earth in the flesh according to God's plan. Galatians 4:4–5 tells us, "When the fullness of time had come, God sent forth His Son, born of a woman, born under the law, to redeem those who were under the law." God's plan for all mankind is through Jesus Christ and Him alone. You may be thinking: Why is Jesus only written about in the New Testament? He can be found throughout the Old Testament because He is the focus of all the Bible. God uses His Word to let mankind know all things; there is no mystery. Jesus Christ is revealed to us in the very first chapter of the Bible.

PROPHECY

Prophecy is the word used in the Bible to foretell the future. Bible scholars tell us there are over 300 scripture references about Christ's birth, life, crucifixion, and resurrection in the Old Testament. Prophecy is defined as a prediction, an inspired utterance of a prophet viewed as a declaration of divine will. It is used to reveal the will or message of God. The revelation can be written or spoken.[11] Jesus Christ was first foretold about prophetically in Genesis 3:15. In Exodus 4:15, God tells Moses, "I will be with your mouth and with his mouth, and I will teach you what you shall do." God instructed the prophets. Prophecy is like a map with danger signals along the way to guide us. If we do not heed the warning signs, we face the future unprepared for what will happen.

Prophecy also proclaimed that a Savior was coming through Jesus Christ. Isaiah 42:9 says, "The former things have come to pass, and new things I declare; before they spring forth I tell you of them." In 2 Peter 1:19,

---

[11] "Prophecy," *The American Heritage Dictionary of the English Language.*

we read, "We have the prophetic word confirmed, which you do well to heed as a light that shines in a dark place." However, John 1:5 says, "And the light shines in the darkness, and the darkness did not comprehend it." The Savior of all mankind came to earth, but most people did not know Him. Isaiah 53:12 says Christ was looked upon as a man, a transgressor of the law. Sinful man did not see Him as God.

God's plan to redeem all men is through Jesus Christ. God knew mankind would fall and need help along the way of life. He saw a need the people had, and there was no intercessor between man and God. Because God is spirit, man felt out of touch with Him. However, it was God who provided a means to reconcile mankind back to Him. Jesus Christ is that link. He is also the Savior for all men. Isaiah 60:16 says, "I the LORD am your Savior and your Redeemer." Hosea 13:4 says, "I am the LORD your God . . . you shall know no God but Me; for there is no savior besides Me."

Throughout mankind's journey in life, he will sin. He is born with a sin nature and is easily enticed to sin. God, in His foreknowledge, knew man's needs. God took on flesh and blood and became man's intercessor to Him. Furthermore, He became man's Redeemer and Savior. From the foundations of the world, the hope for all mankind is through Jesus Christ.

However, God's plan to save man would not start as someone sitting on a throne. He would begin life as all mankind does. How could it be that the Savior of all human life would begin as a newborn baby? It had to be that way in order to fulfill every planned detail of God, the master designer.

QUESTIONS FOR REFLECTION

1. According to Isaiah 59:16, why do we need an intercessor?
2. How does the prophecy concerning Jesus in the Old Testament help to strengthen your faith in a God who sees and knows all?
3. How does it make you feel knowing God planned ahead of time to accommodate for your sin and disobedience? Write out your gratitude for this provision.

FOR UNTO US, A CHILD IS BORN: MAN'S REDEMPTION BEGINS

The Lord himself will give you a sign: Behold, the virgin shall conceive and bear a Son, and shall call His name Emmanuel.
—ISAIAH 7:14

You have already read that prophecy in the Bible was used to tell mankind about the future. Emmanuel means "God is with us," and Isaiah says the Messiah, the Savior, is to be born. He shall be born of a virgin, showing God's power and purity, which would happen 500 years later. The deliverance of the Jewish people was promised: God would take on human flesh in Jesus Christ.

In Isaiah 9:6–7, we read, "For unto us a Child is born; unto us a Son is given; and the government will be upon His shoulder. And His name will be called Wonderful, Counselor, Mighty God, Everlasting Father, Prince of Peace. Of the increase of His government and peace, there will be no end." He will establish His kingdom with justice and judgment. The zeal of the Lord of hosts will perform this. He will be all God and all man in the same body, two natures. God would have a physical body and walk on earth the same as everyone who has ever lived. He would dwell among us for our knowledge and good, an example of how we are to live. He is Wonderful in that God and man are in the same body. He is the greatest

Counselor man could have *if* man would seek Him. He is the Mighty God, for there is no other God. He is the Everlasting Father, for there is no end of His kingdom. For He Himself is our peace (Ephesians 2:14). There is no real peace for man apart from God because the peace of God passes all understanding (Philippians 4:7).

Matthew 1 and Luke 1 give mankind the knowledge of how Jesus Christ would come forth to earth as a child. God sent His angel Gabriel to tell Mary that she would be His mother (Luke 1:26). In verse 27, we read that Mary was a virgin espoused to Joseph, and she was of the royal lineage of David, the second king of Israel. The name Mary means "exalted"—she was highly favored of God. She was a special person chosen by God to become the mother of our Savior, Jesus Christ. In Luke 1:28, we see the Lord was with her and that she was blessed among women.

In Matthew 1:18, we again read Mary was espoused to Joseph. She was contracted to Joseph or, in the present language, engaged to him. But they had not yet come together. Mary was pregnant, and the child was of the Holy Spirit. Mary knew of her own innocence in a time when she could have been looked upon as a harlot. The Jewish custom of the time was that they would be espoused before they would come together; there was a waiting period. Mary was with a child, not of man. The human nature of Christ was not from man but from God. Christ's nature was from the Holy Spirit, which is without sin. Joseph, by law, could have put Mary away. But he was a just man, and the angel of God instructed him to not be afraid to take Mary as his wife. We read further in verse 23: "The virgin shall be with child and bear a Son, and they shall call His name Immanuel," which is translated "God with us." In verse 21, we read, "And she will bring forth a Son, and you shall call His name JESUS, for He will save His people from their sins." Luke 1:32 says, "He will be great, and will be called the Son of the Highest." Verse 33 continues with the proclamation that His kingdom will have no end. Micah 5:2 says Christ will come forth "from of old, from everlasting."

When Mary was told by Gabriel that she would conceive and bear a child, she was troubled. In her innocence, she knew she was untouched by man and considered pure. In Luke 1:34, she asks Gabriel, "How can this be, since I do not know a man?" He responds to her in verse 35, "The Holy Spirit will come upon you, and the power of the Highest will overshadow you." It is the Holy Spirit who sanctifies, for this child shall be holy from God. Jesus Christ would dwell in Mary's womb, holy and pure from God. In the womb, the Son of God transcends into flesh and is born.

In Ecclesiastes 11:5, we read, "As you do not know what is the way of the wind, or how the bones grow in the womb of her who is with child, so you do not know the works of God who makes everything." Through Jesus, man could be brought back to God. It was God's plan to reach down to man, not man reaching up to God. In Luke 1:37, we see, "For with God nothing will be impossible." In verse 38, Mary says to Gabriel, "Let it be to me according to your word." Mary humbled herself and was obedient to God's will.

GOD IN HUMAN FLESH

In Luke 2:1–40, we read about the birth and first few days of Christ's life. In verse 11, we read, "For there is born to you this day in the city of David a Savior, who is Christ the Lord." This day was the day in which Christ came forth, born of woman to be the Savior of the world. It was the exact time in God's plan as promised from everlasting. In verse 31, we see God prepared Christ, and God was manifested in the flesh to all peoples. Jesus came to earth humbly as a baby born in a stable. How could it be the Son of God, pure and holy, would come into the world this way for all mankind? How could the Creator of all things come to man as a baby born in a stable? Why would God do this? There was a reason, and the Bible gives us all the answers.

In Philippians 2:7, we read that Christ was made in the likeness of man, yet God fully dwelt in his body. Christ voluntarily assumed human nature, but His holiness was covered with flesh. Only a few people could see that He was God because He put on the raggedy sin nature of man. He humbled himself in the form of a servant so He could minister to all people. He grew up alongside his earthly father, who was a carpenter. There was nothing about Him that was desired. In Isaiah 53:2, the Bible says, "He shall grow up before Him as a tender plant, and as a root out of dry ground. He has no form or comeliness; and when we see Him, there is no beauty that we would desire Him." People saw Him as a mere sinful man born of Joseph. He laid aside His glory while on earth in the flesh. Christ did reveal His glory to a few people: John the Baptist and the apostles Peter, James, and John saw His glory on earth when Jesus was baptized (Matthew 3:16–17) and on the Mount of Transfiguration (Matthew 17:1–4).

Jesus chose to be made in the likeness of man even though He was without sin and knew no sin. He was with sinful man and was put into prison with the transgressors of the law. He was like every person on earth. He had a physical body, was subject to man's sorrows, and was treated as a sinner. He was like man in everything except He knew no sin. Isaiah 53:3–6 says He was despised and rejected of man, a man of sorrows and acquainted with grief. He was bruised for our iniquities, and the Lord laid on Him the iniquity of all people.

In 1 Timothy 3:16, we read: "Great is the mystery of godliness," in that God was manifest in the flesh. Jesus Christ's character in human flesh was godliness. He was all human, and He was all God. The Spirit of God was in Him at the same time that He had a visible human body. He existed as a person distinct from God the Father and the Holy Spirit. He was seen, heard, and felt. Hebrews 2:16 says Christ took on the seed of Abraham, not the nature of angels. Abraham was born of woman, the sin nature of all human flesh. Christ also was born of woman, but His lineage was of God. Although Christ became human flesh when He was born, He already existed. He has existed for all eternity. He was promised to the Jews, the seed of Abraham. He had heavenly seed and human parents, resulting in two distinct natures. Because He took on the nature of man, He could be like His brethren in all ways except sin (Hebrews 2:17). Hebrews 2:18 tells us Christ was tempted yet did not sin. Christ knows that man is tempted, but we have an Advocate to turn to when trials come our way.

Being the Son of God did not exempt Christ from suffering. Furthermore, as God's Son, He was obedient to God's will and not His own. By His obedience to death on the cross, He became the author of eternal life. As He obeyed God's will, we must obey Christ by faith to live eternally with Him someday (Hebrews 5:8-9).

ETERNAL ONE

According to Scripture, there are two people in the Bible who never died—Elijah (2 Kings 2) and Enoch (Genesis 5:22-35)—but they were still not there in the beginning when God created the world. Jesus Christ was born of the Virgin Mary, but He was without father or mother. There was none before Him, neither was there beginning of days nor end of life (Hebrews 7:3). God has always existed; one of His names is "The Great I AM." In Hebrews 7:16, we read that Christ came forth, not according to the law of the flesh but according to the power of an endless life. In Hebrews 9:11, we see Christ was not made or conceived by anything man did, not with man's hands or abilities. Christ was conceived in the Virgin Mary by the Holy Spirit. He was perfect because God is perfect. He had to be perfect to fulfill God's plan to redeem man from his sin and provide a means for man to come back to Him. In all of God's majesty and wonder, He gave man a Savior wrapped in swaddling clothes lying in a manger.

Throughout the Old Testament of the Bible, prophecy tells us that the Messiah, our Savior, is coming. He will not be like other people. There was something about Jesus that drew people to Him. Luke 2:9 tells us the glory of the Lord shined all around Christ when He was born. In Luke 2:13, we read that there were a multitude of heavenly hosts praising God at that time. What was it about God's glory that drew people to Him or caused awe or fear in others?

Early in the Bible, we see the glory of God. Exodus 24:16–17 tells us the glory of the Lord lived on Mt. Sinai and covered the mountain as a cloud. The sight of the cloud was like consuming fire in the eyes of the people who looked upon it. Everyone knew God was there. In verse 18, we read that Moses spent forty days and forty nights with God on that mountain, and his desire was to see God's glory. In Exodus 33:20, God tells Moses, "You cannot see My face; for no man shall see Me, and live." Then, in verse 23, God tells him, "Then I will take away My hand, and you shall see My back; but My face shall not be seen." God can be seen in all His creation, but man cannot see Him. When Moses came down from the mountain, his skin shined as a bright light. Being in the presence of God changed his physical appearance! When all the people saw him, they were afraid (Exodus 34:29–30). Moses was not aware that he was different. If we spend time alone with God, we, too, will be different. Being in the presence of God and His glory will change us to be more like Him and less like mankind.

God's glory was present when the Jewish people completed the tabernacle in the desert and when Solomon completed the temple. In Psalm 19:1, we read, "The heavens declare the glory of God; and the firmament shows His handiwork." When Christ was born in Bethlehem, all those around saw the glory of God, and some were afraid (Luke 2:9). When in the presence of holiness, righteousness, and a heavenly light, man *should* be afraid. Prophecy tells us in Isaiah 40:5 that the glory of the Lord shall be revealed, and all flesh will see it. The reason man does not see God in creation is because man chooses not to see Him. All the majesty and glory of God was there where Jesus was born. Everything about His character was manifested in Jesus when He took on flesh as a newborn baby. Even though He was just a small baby, God informed the world that this baby was different: "For there is born to you this day in the city of David a Savior, who is Christ the Lord" (Luke 2:11).

WISE MEN

When Christ was born in Bethlehem, wise men from the East were guided by a star to where the baby lay. When they saw Jesus, they fell down and worshipped Him. When in the presence of the earthly king Herod, they did not fall down, nor did they worship him. Have you ever thought about why these wise men fell down and worshipped a baby? This baby could not hurt them, yet they did not worship an earthly king who could have had them slain. These wise men knew this baby was God in flesh and blood. They knew this little baby had far more authority and power than any earthly king. They presented Jesus with gifts of gold, frankincense, and myrrh (Matthew 2:2–11). In Isaiah 60:6, prophecy tells us wise men would come to see Jesus bringing gifts: The multitudes of camels and dromedaries of the East shall come and bring gold and incense and shall proclaim the praises to the Lord.

In all the time that you have heard and read about the birth of Christ, have you ever thought about the types of gifts Jesus received? Why were these the gifts chosen by wise men to give to a baby? Gold is a precious metal that is valued highly; it lasts and is beautiful to look upon. Gold is also given to kings or royalty. John tells us in Revelation 21:10–21 that in eternity, the Holy City of Jerusalem will descend out of heaven, having the glory of God, and its streets will be pure gold. Gold was a valuable gift to give to a newborn baby, who would be the one and only king in eternity. These wise men knew Jesus would someday be King.

He was also given frankincense, a token of worship and an offering to honor God. They knew this child was God in human flesh. In Exodus 30:34–37, Moses is told by God to take sweet spices with pure frankincense and make a perfume, for it shall be pure and holy to the Lord. The Bible tells us in Leviticus 24:7 to use pure frankincense for a memorial, an offering made by fire unto the Lord. Frankincense was given to Christ to worship Him, for He is God.

The last gift given to Jesus was unique in that myrrh was used at the time to prepare a body for burial. The Bible says in John 19:39–40 that Nicodemus brought a mixture of myrrh and aloes and took the body of Jesus. He wound His body with linen clothes and spices. This was the way in which Jews buried their dead at the time. Why would you give myrrh to a newborn baby? They knew that this baby was born to suffer and die.

They knew this baby would someday be King, and He was worthy of worship. They also knew He would die for the sins of all mankind. God revealed to these wise men this baby was God, and He was different from all other babies that had lived. When we look at Christ's birth, life, death, and resurrection, we see God had a plan from the beginning. That plan provided a means for man to come back to Him through a baby, through Jesus Christ and Him only.

These wise men from the East knew something was different about this situation because a star guided them to where the baby Jesus lay. When Christ was born, there was little to be heard from the people. Even though prophecy had told the people a Savior was coming, few people knew Jesus was the Messiah. When John the Baptist first saw Jesus, he said, "Behold! The Lamb of God who takes away the sin of the world!" (John 1:29). He knew who Jesus was, without ever seeing Him. However, the multitudes followed Christ for the miracles He did. They sought the temporal things of the body, not the eternal things of the soul.

Christ was born flesh and blood but was conceived of the Holy Ghost. In God's providential plan, Christ took on the sins of all mankind. God turned His back to Christ when He died on the cross. The holy and righteous God did not and will not look upon sin. God in the flesh, Jesus Christ, took all the sins of the world to the cross and covered them there with His blood. The wise men knew the baby Jesus was Lord and King. He was worthy of honor, praise, and worship.

QUESTION FOR REFLECTION

Something to think about if you have questions about how life began: With God's creation, man is the focal point of everything that exists. Furthermore, God had your heart and soul in mind in everything He has done. With all other theories of life, man is nobody. Do you still believe man evolved?

IT IS THE BLOOD THAT MAKES ATONEMENT FOR THE SOUL: THE CROSS, IT HAD TO BE

And according to the law almost all things are purified with blood, and without shedding of blood there is no remission.
—HEBREWS 9:22

From the beginning of man's life on earth, blood has been shed. Animal sacrifices were used to cover the sins of mankind. When Adam and Eve sinned in the Garden of Eden, God clothed them with animal skins to cover their nakedness (Genesis 3:21). Before there was sin, there was no shame or guilt. There was only the innocence of being with God in Paradise. God killed animals to cover Adam and Eve's nakedness. The innocent were slain for the guilty. Until Christ came, there had been animal sacrifices, the shedding of blood, to atone for man's sins. Hebrews 9:22 says that without the shedding of blood, there is no remission of sins. It was God's way for man to come back to Him. The animal had to be without spot or blemish—perfect—to pardon the sin of the people (Exodus 12:3–13). The blood of the lamb was placed on the doorposts of the Jewish people's homes. If the blood was not there, the death angel would kill all the firstborns who lived in that house. This was

God's plan for man to live by. Innocent lambs would be sacrificed so their blood could atone for man's sins.

ATONEMENT

The high priest was the only person of all the Jewish people who could atone for the people. In Leviticus 16:30, we read that once a year, the high priest would make an atonement to cleanse man from his sins. Atonement is defined as "to repair an injury, to amend or reconcile,"[12] and this was God's way of reconciling man back to Him when he sinned. God wanted His people to be clean from their sins. The high priest had to bring blood for himself to cover his sins before he could make an offering for the people. The high priest was human like all other people. He, too, was born with a sin nature. The service was holy unto God, an offering unto Him. In Hebrews 10:3, we read that when the high priest sacrificed animals every year, it was in remembrance of man's sins. Hebrews 10:4 reads, "For it is not possible that the blood of bulls and goats could take away sins." Animal blood is not the same as human blood. Furthermore, it was man who sinned, not animals.

Animal blood never satisfied God's penalty for mankind's sin. Even though the animals were spotless, the sins of man could only be pushed forward another year—that is until Jesus Christ would come forth. It was Adam and Eve and all mankind who sinned against God (Genesis 3:15–19). That is why there had to be perfect human blood to meet God's criteria for the atonement of all mankind's sins. The blood of Christ, a perfect human without spot or blemish, finally satisfied God's divine judgment for the sins of man.

Hebrews 10:1 tells us that the yearly practice of the high priest was a shadow of things to come later. Those sacrifices done once every year could never make man perfect or take away his sins. If this practice had made man clean before God, the practice would continue today (10:2). All the

---

[12] "Atonement," *The American Heritage Dictionary of the English Language.*

sacrifice did was to make remembrance of the sins and push them forward another year (10:3). When Jesus Christ came into the world, He did not bring sacrifices and offerings as the high priest did in the previous years. He brought His body, which was prepared by God for this time. Christ's body was to be the sacrifice. His body and blood were perfect, without spot or blemish. He was the innocent Lamb. Human blood and a human body were required to atone for man and reconcile him back to God. The shedding of Christ's blood met God's requirements for the atonement of mankind's sins forever. In Hebrews 10:10–18, we read that those who believe are sanctified and cleansed through the offering of Christ, once and for all. Every year, the priests made an offering to God that never could, nor ever would, take away man's sin. "For by one offering He has perfected forever those who are being sanctified" (10:14). The Bible tells us in verse 18 that now, where there is remission for sin, there is no longer an offering needed for sin. God's plan to redeem man was finished. There is nothing man can do or has to do to atone for his sins; Christ has paid the price in full.

Every detail in God's plan came to pass. You may ask: Why would God send forth His Son to endure such pain and agony? Throughout the Bible, it is God who reaches out to man. In John 12:27, Jesus was troubled at the thought of His death. He did not want to suffer and die on the cross. However, He was willing and obedient to die for the sins of all mankind. Jesus Christ had an appointment with death on the cross: "But for this purpose I came to this hour." For you, me, and all mankind is why Christ was willing to die.

It was no accident or mistake that Christ went to the cross and died. All that is written about God's love is very true. However, His greatest attribute is His holiness. Any sin separates man from God. In Hebrews 9:26, the Bible says that from the foundation of the world, Christ has come forth to suffer and put away sin by the sacrifice of Himself. From the beginning, God knew man would sin. Furthermore, the sting of sin is death. There is God's law and man's free will to choose what he wants to do. Everyone knows right and wrong. The penalty of sin and death no longer exists for those who believe in Christ. In the fullness of time, God sent forth His Son to bring mankind back to Him. From the foundation of the world, God's plan and purposes for man continue and will continue until the end of time. Until that time, man has a choice. Christ has paid the sin debt for everyone who chooses to believe in Him. Those who choose not to believe will someday pay their own sin debt. God gave everyone that free will.

QUESTION FOR REFLECTION

If everything we do in life is positive, why do we try to amend relationships with people?

I AM COME THAT THEY MIGHT HAVE LIFE: HOPE AND ETERNITY

I have come that they may have life, and that they may have it more abundantly. I am the good shepherd. The good shepherd gives His life for the sheep.

—JOHN 10:10–11

When Christ came to earth, He was the Son of God. But He came to earth to show man a different side of God. We read in Galatians 4:4, "In the fullness of time, God sent forth his Son born of woman, born under the law. In God's timing, He sent Jesus to be with man because God knew man's heart.

When you look at the life Christ lived, you see He was more than a Savior to man. He was every role model man needed to live before God and other people.

What can we learn from looking at Christ's life as a human that will help us throughout our lives? I looked at many different roles Christ lived during His life while on earth.

SAVIOR

Jesus is called the Savior to all mankind in many verses of the Bible. The dictionary defines a savior as a person who rescues another person.[13] Before Jesus was born, the Bible says that Mary would "bring forth a Son, and you shall call His name JESUS, for He will save His people from their sins" (Matthew 1:21). Luke 2:11 says, "For there is born to you this day in the city of David a Savior, who is Christ the Lord." In John 4:42, the people knew Jesus was the Savior of the world when they heard Him speak. I believe the wise men knew Jesus was born to save all mankind. "For to us a Savior is born"—Jesus Christ came to take away the sins of the world.

REDEEMER

Jesus is also called man's Redeemer in the Bible. A redeemer is someone who recovers ownership of another person.[14] He pays off someone to fulfill a promise and set you free. Isaiah 47:4 says, "Our Redeemer, the Lord of hosts is His name, the Holy One of Israel." Jesus tells us when the last days are come to "look up and lift up your heads, because your redemption draws near" (Luke 21:28). In Titus 2:14, we read that Christ "gave Himself for us, that He might redeem us from every lawless deed and purify for Himself His own special people, zealous for good works." Jesus redeemed us when He died on the cross and rose again.

HIGH PRIEST

Christ lived before man as our High Priest. A priest is someone who delivers or gives religious or moral instructions to man.[15] In Isaiah 61:1–3, we read that Isaiah was to console those who mourn, to give them beauty for ashes, the garment of praise for the spirit of heaviness, and to proclaim liberty to those in bondage. Isaiah also says He will bring comfort, that

---

[13] "Savior," *American Heritage Dictionary of the English Language.*

[14] "Redeem," *American Heritage Dictionary of the English Language.*

[15] "Priest," *The Pictorial Bible Dictionary.*

the people "may be called trees of righteousness" planted by the Lord. Hebrews 2:17 tells us Christ was made like His brethren in all things that he might be a merciful and faithful High Priest. In Hebrews 4:15, we see Christ is a High Priest we can reach out to with our problems. He was tempted in all areas of life as we are but without sin. In Hebrews 9:11–12, we read that Christ is a High Priest not born of man but by the shedding of His perfect blood. He entered the Most Holy Place once for all, having obtained eternal redemption.

INTERCESSOR, MEDIATOR

Jesus Christ lived as our intercessor to God. An intercessor is a mediator, someone who brings two sides together.[16] Ephesians 2:15–16 says Christ replaced in His flesh the enemy, even the law, which did not bring man to God. What the law could not do, Christ could in reconciling man back to God, ending the separation between man and God. Mankind did not reach up to God; He reached down to man.

Mediator is similar to *intercessor*: someone who goes before two or more parties to bring about a settlement.[17] It is a means to reconcile the parties back to each other. In 1 Timothy 2:5, the Bible says, "For there is one God and one Mediator between God and men, the Man Christ Jesus." In Galatians 3:19, we read that God's law was given to man because of man's sin "till the Seed should come to whom the promise was made." Christ came forth as promised to be man's Mediator. Therefore, He is able to save all those who come to God because He lives to make intercession between man and God (Hebrews 7:25). God saw that man could not come to Him because He is holy. But God provided a way for man to come back to Him through Christ's blood, which covers man's sin. When God looks at Christians, He sees Christ's blood, not mankind's sin. All people have a Mediator who allows us back in fellowship with God through Jesus Christ if we choose to believe.

---

[16] "Intercessor," *The Pictorial Bible Dictionary.*
[17] "Mediator," *The Pictorial Bible Dictionary.*

SERVANT

Although Christ is God, and someday He will be King, He was humble and willing to be a servant before His apostles. A servant is someone who is submissive or is employed to serve others.[18] In Philippians 2:7, the Bible says Christ "made Himself of no reputation, taking the form of a bond-servant, and coming in the likeness of men." In Matthew 12:18, we read, "Christ is God's chosen servant and he will declare justice to the Gentiles." In Colossians 3:22, we are given instructions on how to live as bondservants. We are to obey our masters in all things according to the flesh, not with eye service, as men-pleasers, but in sincerity of heart, fearing God. In Colossians 4:1, we read, "Masters, give your bondservants what is just and fair, knowing that you also have a Master in heaven." Christ was a very humble person while He lived on earth before others. Romans 6:16 says, "To whom you present yourselves slaves to obey, you are that one's slaves." You can obey your sin object unto death or walk in obedience to God to righteousness and eternal life. We all serve something in some capacity; will you be a servant unto life or death? Christ was obedient to God to go to the cross and die for the sins of the world. Everyone who has ever come to Christ humbled himself before God. If you are too proud to be a servant to God, you will never see the kingdom of heaven.

FRIEND

Christ was a friend to all those He was around. A friend is a favored companion to us or a trusted comrade.[19] In Proverbs 17:17, we read, "A friend loves at all times." If you have friends, you have to show yourself as friendly to others (Proverbs 18:24). In Luke 7:34, Jesus was described as a friend to tax collectors and sinners. John 15:12–15 tells us that we are to love one another as Christ has loved us, for greater love has no man than to lay down his life for his friends. Christ tells those who follow Him they are not

---

[18] "Servant," *American Heritage Dictionary of the English Language.*
[19] "Friend," *American Heritage Dictionary of the English Language.*

servants but friends because they are willing to obey God's commands. If we are going to be friends with Christ, we have to be obedient to His Word.

DOOR

As we look further at the roles Jesus lived while on earth, we see He was also the door: an "access or passage to something" or "to close off that means to something."[20] In John 10:9, we read that Jesus is the door for the sheep: "If anyone enters by Me, he will be saved." Acts 14:27 shows us how the Jews realized God had opened the door of faith to the Gentiles. In Revelation 3:8, Jesus says, "I have set before you an open door, and no one can shut it." In Revelation 3:20, Jesus tells everyone that He stands at the door and knocks, and if anyone hears His voice and opens the door, He will come into him. Christ is the only door, and He is seeking anyone who will open their heart's door to let Him in. Jesus said in John 14:6, "I am the way, the truth, and the life. No one comes to the Father except through Me." When God instructed Noah to build the ark, there was only one door to get on and off. God is standing at the door. He will let you in if you seek Him with all your heart. The only obstacle keeping you away from that door is your unbelief. It is your decision to make.

TRUE VINE

In John 15:1, Jesus tells us, "I am the true vine, and My Father is the vine-dresser." The dictionary defines a vine as a flexible stem that grows from the ground.[21] It has a root source to grow from. Jesus Christ is man's only source of strength and sustenance to live. John 15:4 says we must abide in Christ, and He abides in us." The branch or stem cannot bear fruit of itself except if it abides in the vine or root. Man cannot live apart from God. God created man; therefore, only God knows what man needs to live. The stem cannot live apart from the true vine. The Bible says man will have

[20] "Door," *American Heritage Dictionary of the English Language.*
[21] "Vine," *American Heritage Dictionary of the English Language.*

everything he needs in life if he will be obedient to God's plan for his life: "So if you walk in My ways, to keep My statutes and My commandments, as your father David walked, then I will lengthen your days" (1 Kings 3:14). Even though God is spirit, He is the living God.

GOD AND JESUS

Many people in this world believe there is a God, but there are those who do not believe that Jesus is God. They believe Jesus and God are two distinct, different beings. The dictionary defines God in two different ways. First, God is a being of supernatural powers or attributes believed in or worshipped by people. He controls everything and is idolized as God. Second, God is conceived as the perfect omnipotent, omniscient originator and ruler of the universe. He is the principle object of faith and worship in monotheistic religions. God is the force, effect, or manifestation of man's being that explains the world in which he lives. Jesus is the Son of Mary and founder of Christianity. He is also called the Son of God, the Messiah, and Jesus Christ. He is the Anointed and was foretold by the prophets in the Old Testament. Christ is further described as the divine manifestation of God.

In John 10:30, Jesus said, "I and My Father are one." Jesus tells us in John 13:20, "He who receives Me receives Him who sent Me." In John 14:9, Jesus tells Phillip, "He who has seen Me has seen the Father." Colossians 2:9 says, "For in Him dwells all the fullness of the Godhead bodily." The Bible is plain in stating Jesus Christ is God, and God dwells in Him. There are many verses in the Book of John that say Jesus Christ is God. God took on flesh and blood and became Jesus Christ to allow mankind access back to Him.

THE BREAD OF LIFE

Jesus is described in the Bible as the bread of life. Life is the property or quality manifested in functions such as metabolism, growth, reproduction, and response to stimulation.[22] Bread is a food that is necessary for life. In John 6:48, Jesus says, "I am the bread of life," and in John 6:35, He says, "He who comes to Me shall never hunger, and he who believes in Me shall never thirst." Christ tells His followers in John 6:49–50, "Your fathers ate the manna in the wilderness and are dead. This is the bread which comes from heaven, that one may eat of it and not die." Jesus tells them He is the "living bread" (6:51). Bread will help man to sustain life, but it will not meet all of his needs. In Luke 4:4, Jesus tells the people, "Man shall not live by bread alone, but by every word of God." If all we take into our bodies is food to nourish the body, we will sustain physical life. However, our souls will die.

SHEPHERD OF THE SHEEP

Sheep and shepherds are written about 227 times in the Bible.[23] Of all the animals God created, sheep are the most noted. Does that create any interest in you as to why? Sheep need someone to care for them—a shepherd. A shepherd is one who guards or cares for sheep and also one who cares for a group of people.[24] The Bible says in Numbers 27:16–17 that someone was set over the people to go in and out from them. That person led the people because they were as sheep without a shepherd. In Isaiah 40:11, we read, "He will feed His flock like a shepherd; He will gather the lambs with His arm, and carry them in His bosom, and gently lead those who are with young." When the sheep have no shepherd, they scatter and become meat for the beasts of the field (Ezekiel 34:5). Ezekiel 34:23 says, "I will establish one shepherd over them, and he shall feed them." Jesus tells us about the role of the shepherd in John 10:1–2: "I say to you, he who does not enter the sheepfold by the door, but climbs up some other way, the same is a thief and robber. But he who enters through the door is

---

[22] "Life," *American Heritage Dictionary of the English Language.*

[23] James Strong, LLD, STD, *The Strongest Strong's Concordance* (Grand Rapids, MI: Zondervan, 2001).

[24] "Shepherd," *American Heritage Dictionary of the English Language.*

the shepherd of the sheep." In verses 4 through 5, Jesus says that He goes before the sheep, and they follow Him because they know His voice. They will not follow a stranger and will flee from him, for they do not know the voice of strangers. Jesus sums up His role as our shepherd in verses 7 and 11 when He says He is the door and the Good Shepherd. "The good shepherd gives His life for the sheep."

Man will travel many roads in life, seeking the answers to life. He will often follow any path, not knowing where that road will lead him. The Bible teaches us there is only one road and one Shepherd who can lead us safely and happily to our destination. That Shepherd is Jesus Christ.

Throughout the Bible, people are written about as sheep. Why is it the Bible equates man with sheep? I believe the reason is that mankind's behavior is much like sheep. Sheep are timid, meek, submissive, quiet, gentle, fearful, and easily panicked. Some people say sheep are dumb and gullible. They group together, mob-like. They try to flee from danger, stampede easily, and are vulnerable to prey. They have little means of self-defense and will follow someone they perceive as a friend. They are inclined to follow a leader. If they fall, they cannot get back up of their own will. They cannot clean themselves when they get dirty. Sheep need the most care of all the animals in God's creation. Sheep are always led; they are never driven.

Jesus says mankind needs a shepherd to lead us. God is telling us that man does not know where he is going. In Matthew 9:36, we read that Jesus had compassion for the people because they were as sheep without a shepherd.

Mankind claims to be intelligent beings, but why does our behavior repeat itself over and over again? In 1978, in Jonestown, Guyana, 900 people followed Jim Jones to their deaths. In 1993, 76 people followed David Koresh to their deaths in Waco, Texas. Every year, when professional teams win a championship, people riot and destroy private property. Most of these people, individually, are probably quiet and peaceful. Why do they become mob-like and destroy property? They follow a leader; they are not driven to break the law. They do not think about the direction they are going; they just follow someone. Why does history repeat itself? Who or what is leading you in the direction you are taking in life?

In Psalm 95:7, we read, "He is our God, and we are the people of His pasture, and the sheep of His hand." In Jeremiah 50:6, the Bible says, "My people have been lost sheep. Their shepherds have led them astray." Every step you take in life requires a decision. Are you timid, fearful, gullible, and easily deceived? Are you following someone who does not know where he is going? The Bible tells us that it is not in man to know where he is going (Jeremiah 10:23). Jesus Christ is the Good Shepherd, and He gave His life for all mankind. He will guide you and me to living waters of life. Who is your guide?

TEACHER

Multitudes of people followed Jesus wherever He went. He often took the time to teach them. A teacher is defined as someone who teaches or imparts knowledge or skills to someone.[25] A teacher gives instructions in a manner that learning is fostered by example. In Judges 13:8, Manoah, Samson's father, asked that the man of God teach his parents how to raise their child. In 1 Samuel 12:23, Samuel says he will teach the people the good and right way. In Job 27:11, we see that Job wanted to be taught about the hand of God. David asks the Lord in Psalm 27:11, "Teach me Your way, O LORD, and lead me on a smooth path, because of my enemies." In Isaiah 2:3, we read that we are to go to the house of God, for He will teach us His ways, and we shall walk in His paths.

In Mark 4:1, Jesus was teaching by the seaside. He had to enter a small boat to teach from because of the multitudes of people who were on the seashore. Nicodemus, a ruler of the Jewish people, came to Jesus. He knew Jesus was a teacher who came from God, for no one could do these signs unless God was with Him (John 3:1–2). Before Jesus was crucified and ascended to heaven, He told His followers, "The Helper, the Holy Spirit,

---

[25] "Teacher," *The Pictorial Bible Dictionary.*

whom the Father will send in My name, He will teach you all things" (John 14:26). The Helper is the Holy Spirit of God, and He indwells the heart of all believers and teaches or guides believers to walk as God directs them. We are commanded to teach others and to live as an example of Jesus before all people.

ADVOCATE

It is reassuring to know that we have an Advocate in Christ while we live. An advocate is someone who pleads or argues for a cause on behalf of others. He supports, defends, and gives evidence for you.[26] Jesus tells us in John 14:16 that He will send believers another Helper that He may abide with us forever. The Holy Spirit or Helper is an Advocate of God. The Helper consoles, strengthens, helps, counsels, guides, teaches, directs, and does so many other things for believers as an Advocate of God. In 1 John 2:1, we are instructed to not sin. If we do sin, however, we have an Advocate with the Father, Jesus Christ the Righteous. The Holy Spirit is part of the Trinity of God. Believers have an Advocate who indwells our souls wherever we go and whatever the circumstances of life present.

OBEDIENT TO THE FATHER

Jesus was obedient on earth, even to His death on the cross. If Jesus is God, why would He suffer and die an agonizing death on the cross? If Jesus is the Son of God, why would He need to be obedient to anyone? Obedience is defined in the dictionary as submitting to authority and carrying out a command.[27] It requires you to be under the control of another as a soldier in the military. Obedience is needed in life, or there will be disorder. In John 6:38, Jesus says, "For I have come down from heaven, not to do My own will, but the will of Him who sent Me." In Philippians 2:8, we read that Jesus humbled Himself and became obedient to death, even the

---

[26] "Advocate," *American Heritage Dictionary of the English Language.*
[27] "Obedience," *American Heritage Dictionary of the English Language.*

death on the cross. Though He was the Son of God, He was obedient to the Father. His obedience to God cost Jesus His life. Romans 5:19 tells us, By one man's disobedience (Adam), many were made sinners, so also by one Man's obedience (Christ), many will be made righteous (parenthetical mine).

Man will obey some sort of laws and rules wherever he lives. God created governments and authority. In Romans 13:1, we read that every person is subject unto higher powers, for there is no power but of God. Governments and authority are everywhere we go. In all of God's creation, there is order; nothing happened randomly or haphazardly. In 1 Corinthians 14:40, the Bible says, "Let all things be done decently and in order." God put order to everything He created. Life requires obedience to our laws and to God's Word, the Bible. If we are not walking in obedience, we will suffer the consequences. That is man's law, and it is God's law.

COUNSELOR

Where there is no counsel, the people fall, but in the multitude of counselors, there is safety (Proverbs 11:14). Jesus was a Counselor to all who came near Him. The dictionary defines a counselor as someone who gives advice; they are an adviser.[28] Guidance is given by someone who is knowledgeable in guiding others in the right direction. In Isaiah 9:6, Christ is called Wonderful, Counselor, and the Mighty God. In Psalm 16:7, the Bible says, "I will bless the LORD who has given me counsel." Jeremiah 32:19 tells us, "You are great in counsel and mighty in work, for Your eyes are open to all the ways of the sons of men." In Isaiah 40:13, the Bible asks, "Who has directed the Spirit of the LORD, or as His counselor has taught Him?" God created man; therefore, we cannot give advice to the Creator. How can man question or advise God? As believers, we have the Holy Spirit dwelling inside our mortal bodies. He can direct us in every step we take in life. Christians have the best counselor there is—if we seek His guidance.

---

[28] "Counselor," *American Heritage Dictionary of the English Language.*

THE WAY

God knows our way because He sees all things. What is the way? The dictionary defines the way as a course affording passage from one place to another.[29] It is a route that progresses in a direction. The way can also be defined as a manner of living your life. In Jeremiah 10:23, the Bible says, "The way of man is not in himself; it is not in man who walks to direct his own steps." In Proverbs 14:12, we read, "There is a way that seems right to a man, but its end is the way of death." Jesus tells His followers in Matthew 7:13–14 that "wide is the gate and broad is the way that leads to destruction, and there are many who go in by it. Because narrow is the gate and difficult is the way which leads to life, and there are few who find it." God's commandments are lamps and lights for man to walk in the way of life (Proverbs 6:23). Psalm 1:6 says, "The Lord knows the way of the righteous, but the way of the ungodly shall perish." Not only does God know the way, but His way is perfect.

There are people who believe there are many ways to get to heaven. But the Bible tells us there is only one way. In John 14:6, Jesus says, "I am the way, the truth, and the life. No one comes to the Father except through Me." John 5:22 says that God has given all judgment to the Son. The Bible is very plain in that Jesus Christ is the only way man will reach the kingdom of heaven. What direction are you taking in life? Do you know the way you are going? Man has a built-in true compass in his soul and spirit. God put it there to guide you the right way—if you allow it to direct you.

TRUTH

What is truth? This is a question many people ask in this day. Some believe truth changes with time, and popular opinion of the day dictates what is true. Others believe there is a standard or set of rules that never changes with time, and truth is relevant regardless of the time. Truth is defined as

---

[29] "Way," *American Heritage Dictionary of the English Language.*

consistency or corresponding to facts and reality.[30] Truth is conforming to logic, knowledge, accuracy, integrity, rules, and standards. Truth is also exact, genuine, and set apart. It is exclusive in that it stands alone from rumors or traditions. Truth can be someone's character: someone who is reliable and has virtue.

Everything Christians believe is based upon the character of God and the Bible. If we cannot believe God is true, there is no foundation to believe anything about God. Many people believe in God, but what about Jesus Christ, the Holy Spirit, and the Bible? I have already stated Jesus Christ is God in the flesh. The Bible says in John 1:1, "In the beginning was the Word, and the Word was with God, and the Word was God." This verse tells us the Bible is true because it has existed from eternity. There is a standard from which all truth is based, and it is in God and the Bible. If you feel you are a truthful person, do you always tell the truth?

In 1 John 2:4, the Bible says that anyone who says he knows God and does not keep His commandments is a liar. The Bible says a liar is someone who denies Jesus is the Christ (1 John 2:22). In 1 John 4:20, we read that any person who says he loves God and hates his brother is a liar. How can we not love our brother whom we have seen and love God whom we have not seen? Psalm 116:11 declares that all people are liars.

If all mankind are liars, how can anyone be saved or inherit the kingdom of God? The Bible tells us whoever continues to live such a lifestyle will not go to heaven. 1 Corinthians 6:11 says, "And such were some of you. But you were washed, but you were sanctified, but you were justified in the name of the Lord Jesus and by the Spirit of our God." The Bible tells us to believe and live the truth.

Truth is a part of God's character. Jeremiah 10:10 says that the Lord is the true and the living God. John 15:1 says, "Jesus is the true vine," and John 7:28 says, "He who sent Me is true." In Psalm 19:9, we read that God's judgments are true and righteous. Psalm 119:160 tells us, "Your word is truth. And every one of Your righteous judgments endures forever." 1 John

---

[30] "Truth," *American Heritage Dictionary of the English Language.*

1:1 says, "That which was from the beginning, which we have heard, which we have seen with our eyes, which we have looked upon, and our hands have handled, concerning the Word of life." John 1:14 says, "The Word became flesh and dwelt among us." From these verses, we know the Bible is true because it is of God and is God.

In 2 Timothy 2:13, the Bible says Christ cannot deny Himself. In Titus 1:2, we read that God cannot lie. When Christ returns, He will be called "faithful and true," for He will judge the world in truth and righteousness. 1 John 2:21 says there is no lie in truth. The Pharisees came to Jesus in Matthew 22:16 and said to Him, "Teacher, we know that You are true, and teach the way of God in truth." The religious leaders of the time of Christ knew He was true. He taught the truth, but they still crucified Him.

By Christ's example and the Bible, we know truth. How should we be living before others? In John 8:31–32, Jesus tells us, "If you abide in My word, you are My disciples indeed. And you shall know the truth, and the truth shall make you free." When you live your life in truth, you never have to fear or worry about others. Lies and deceit foster ill feelings in your heart and soul. John 17:17 says, "Sanctify them by Your truth. Your word is truth." In Ephesians 4:24, we read that we must put on the new man, which was created in holiness and righteousness. In 2 John 4 and 3 John 4, we read that John had no greater joy than to hear that the people walk in truth. In 1 Kings 2:4, the Bible says, "If your sons take heed to their way, to walk before Me in truth with all their heart and with all their soul . . . you shall not lack a man on the throne of Israel." I believe God's Word applies to America as well. There are only blessings from Him if we live in truth before others.

Proverbs 12:17–19 says we are to speak the truth because truth is forever, but a lie is just for a moment. The apostle Paul tells us in Philippians 4:8 that whatsoever things are true, noble, just, pure, lovely, of good report, or any other virtue, we should meditate on these things. In 2 Thessalonians 2:10, the Bible says that the unrighteous will believe lies because they do not want the truth. Are you walking down that path now? Mankind knows the truth, but he would rather live a lie. Every person knows what a lie is, and they know what is true. Truth will set you free because you are not trying to hide anything. You never have to fear or be ashamed when you walk in truth.

SANCTIFIED

Every person is born with a sin nature. How does mankind overcome that nature? Through sanctification, which is defined as to make holy, to practice holiness, or to be sacred.[31] Sanctified means to set apart or belonging to God. The Bible says in Leviticus 11:44, "I am the LORD your God. You shall consecrate [sanctify] yourselves, and you shall be holy; for I am holy" (parenthetical mine). God set apart the high priest from the other priests. He also separated Israel from all other peoples on the earth. God told the Jewish people what was clean and unclean in the food they ate. God has rules and guidelines for people to live by, and they are found in the Bible. Christ's prayer in John 17:17 is that mankind would sanctify themselves through the Bible: "For your Word is truth." 1 Timothy 4:4-5 says that every creature of God is good and can be sanctified through God's Word.

The Bible tells believers to not be unequally yoked with unbelievers (2 Corinthians 6:14), instructing those who believe to not marry unbelievers. God created marriage to be holy; however, man wants to live life his way. But in all areas of life, God has alternative plans for man's disobedience. In 1 Corinthians 7:12–14, the Bible says that the unbelieving partner can be sanctified through the believing spouse. With God, there is always a way to be reconciled back to Him. Sin separates mankind from God, but He reaches out to man to bring him back.

HOPE

What motivates you in life each day? What anchors you to endure the tasks of each day? Is it money, family, power, climbing the ladder of success,

---

[31] "Sanctification," *American Heritage Dictionary of the English Language.*

recognition, self-esteem, or some other factor? Do you have hope for something better someday in life and eternity? Paul tells us in 1 Corinthians 15:19 that "if in this life only we have hope in Christ, we are of all men the most pitiable." I believe Paul is telling us we all should have something or someone to believe in beyond our lifetime. Jesus Christ is our anchor and hope for now and eternity. Hope is being confident, trusting, and looking forward to something with expectation.[32] Faith is essential to having hope because we have to believe in someone. As believers in Christ, that confidence and trust is in Him.

In Psalm 146:5, we read that the man who has hope in God is happy. In Romans 15:13, the Bible tells us God is the source of hope for mankind. In Romans 8:24–25, we see believers are saved by hope. Hope that is seen is not hope. Why would you hope for something you have seen? If we hope for something we don't see, we will have the patience to wait for it. Ephesians 2:12 says all men are without hope until they come to believe in Jesus Christ. Real hope is based in Jesus Christ, not in the heart of man (1 Timothy 1:1). Proverbs 14:32 says the righteous have hope, but the wicked are banished in their wickedness. Where do you look for hope because it does not naturally occur in the heart of man?

In God's foreknowledge, He never left the answers to life for man to stumble across or haphazardly find. Romans 15:4 says, "Whatever things were written before were written for our learning, that we through the patience and comfort of the Scriptures might have hope." For all believers, there is a hope laid up in heaven (Colossians 1:5). In Hebrews 6:19, we read, "This hope we have as an anchor for the soul, both sure and steadfast," is with God. Hope will sustain us through the ups and downs of life. When life's journey is over, 1 Thessalonians 4:13 says that hope in Christ will sustain us through the sorrow of losing someone we love. We are not to sorrow as others who have no hope. Life takes us down many roads, both pleasant and unpleasant. What kind of anchor are you holding onto to get you through life? Through Christ's life and resurrection, there is hope for

---

[32] "Hope," *American Heritage Dictionary of the English Language.*

all who believe. Hope will sustain us when everything in life seems to be going wrong. Jesus Christ is our hope for now and all eternity.

DELIVERER

Believers trust in Christ to deliver us from the judgment of God. In Psalm 56:13, we read, God has delivered my soul from death, and He will keep me from falling. My deliverer will not only welcome me to heaven, but He will deliver me through the trials of life. Who or what is a deliverer? The dictionary defines deliver, deliverance and deliverer as someone who rescues you from bondage or danger. It is further defined as someone who keeps a promise to you. In this life, are there any promises associated with what you believe? The Bible says in Psalm 86:13, Great is Your mercy toward me. And You have delivered my soul from hell. King David said in II Samuel 22:2, "The Lord is my rock and my fortress and my deliverer." Jeremiah 1:8 tells Christians to not be afraid, for I am with you to deliver you. In Isaiah 46:4, the Bible says, I have made you, I will carry you, and I will deliver you. We can hold onto God's promise to deliver us as we walk through this life.

REFUGE

Christians have a refuge to hold onto if the circumstances of life become a problem. What or who is a refuge? The dictionary defines refuge as protection or shelter from danger.[33] In Deuteronomy 33:27, the Bible says the eternal God is our refuge and protector from the enemy. In 2 Samuel 22:3, we read, "The God of my strength, in whom I will trust; my shield and the horn of my salvation, my stronghold and my refuge." Where do you turn for refuge in times of trouble? Psalm 46:1 says God is our refuge and strength when we are in trouble. Psalm 62:8, the Bible says we are to trust God at all times because He is our refuge.

There will be heartaches in life; no one is immune from them. In Job

---

[33] "Refuge," *American Heritage Dictionary of the English Language.*

14:1, the Bible says, "Man who is born of woman is of few days and full of trouble." How will we handle the heartaches of life—because they will come? Will we turn to God or blame Him? Everyone knows God, for He formed us. He should be our refuge in times of storms.

GUIDE

Who do we trust to guide us through life? A guide is someone who shows the way by leading or giving directions.[34] Guides know the course to be pursued, and they lead, direct, or advise us on the paths we need to take. The Bible tells us in Psalm 112:5, "A good man deals graciously and lends; he will guide his affairs with discretion." Solomon says in Proverbs 23:19, "Be wise; and guide your heart in the way."

Do we seek man's wisdom in directing us to what is important in life? The Bible tells us in Psalm 32:8, "I will instruct you and teach you in the way you should go." Isaiah 58:11 says, "The Lord will guide you continually, and satisfy your soul" throughout life.

We don't have to journey through life alone; God knows all about us and the needs we have in life. Jeremiah 10:23 says, "It is not in man who walks to direct his own steps." Are we going through life in our own wisdom? There is a guide who knows the way. Proverbs 1:7 reads, "The fear of the LORD is the beginning of knowledge, but fools despise wisdom and instruction." Would we go through the deepest jungle in Africa without a guide? Each of us must decide the course in life we will take. There will be trials; who will we choose to guide us in life?

PEACE

With all the problems and heartaches in life, where do we go to find peace in our hearts? God knows our thoughts and the heaviness we feel in our hearts. When my heart is very heavy, I can call on God. When I do, there is a peace that floods my soul that cannot be explained. There have been

---

[34] "Guide," *American Heritage Dictionary of the English Language.*

other times in which I have tried to find that peace, but I could not find it. I believe God knows when we really need His peace. What, then, is real peace? Is it something between nations, or is it as simple as being in our hearts? Peace is defined as the freedom from inward or outward disturbance and the absence of war or hostility.[35] It is also an agreement or treaty between two or more parties. Peace is an inner state of contentment, calmness, serenity, or a state of spiritual tranquility.

Ecclesiastes 3:8 says there is "a time to love, and a time to hate; a time of war, and a time of peace." I do not believe there will ever be a time of peace on earth until Christ returns. How can there be peace on earth when mankind cannot find it within his own heart? In Psalm 4:8, we read we can "lie down in peace, and sleep; for You alone, O LORD, make me dwell in safety." Why do those who believe find so much peace in life in a time when there is so much turmoil? As believers, we can have a peace in our hearts when all our external world is in chaos.

In Isaiah 59:8, we read that the wicked do not know the way of peace. Jeremiah 8:15 says, "We looked for peace, but no good came." In Ezekiel 7:25, the Bible tells us destruction will come to the wicked. They will seek peace, but there shall be none. As long as man seeks to live his life apart from God, he will not find peace in his heart and soul. Romans 5:1 tells us, "We have peace with God through our Lord Jesus Christ." Romans 14:17 says, "For the kingdom of God is not eating and drinking, but righteousness and peace and joy in the Holy Spirit." The peace that believers have is through their relationship with Jesus Christ.

Colossians 3:15 says, "Let the peace of God rule in your hearts, to which also you were called in one body." When we are obedient to what God would have us do, He will keep us in perfect peace because our minds are trusting Him all the time (Isaiah 26:3). As I have found, and so many others have found as well, the peace of God surpasses all human understanding (Philippians 4:7). In John 14:27, Jesus tells His disciples, "Peace I leave with you, My peace I give to you; not as the world gives do I give to

---

[35] "Peace," *American Heritage Dictionary of the English Language.*

you. Let not your heart be troubled, neither let it be afraid." We can have an inward peace because of the promises of Jesus Christ.

I have felt in my heart that peace, a peace that is so difficult to explain to others; however, it is so real I want to have it in my heart often. Have you ever had that kind of peace in your heart? Until you have the peace of God, you do not know real peace.

EXAMPLE

I have given you some examples of the roles Christ lived before all mankind during the thirty-three years He was on earth. There are probably many other roles you can think of that I did not include. I have tried to look at roles He lived and not look at His character. However, it is hard to separate one from the other. Furthermore, man, in all his wisdom, will never be able to explain how Christ was all man and all God. He was flesh and blood as we are, yet He had God's nature as well. While on earth, He wanted mankind to see God differently. He wanted to be someone who could see and feel the needs of every person while keeping the holiness of God. In all areas of life, He was an example for us to live: someone worthy of imitation or duplicating.[36] An example is a model of behavior, a pattern to follow, or a precedent in which there is no other. Truly, Christ lived a life before all of us that no other person could have lived.

In John 13:15, Jesus tells us, "I have given you an example, that you should do as I have done to you." Romans 15:4 says the Bible was written for our learning. The apostle Paul tells us in Philippians 3:17 to walk as he has walked before God so that we may be examples to others. In 1 Thessalonians 1:7 and 1 Peter 5:3, we read that we are to live our lives in such a way that we are examples to everyone. The Bible says in 1 Timothy 4:12 that in our youth, we are to be examples in how we talk, how we live, and how we love. We are to live with a spirit of faith and purity. In 2 Corinthians 3:2, the Bible says we are an open letter written, known,

---

[36] "Example," *American Heritage Dictionary of the English Language.*

and read by every person. We may not feel that anyone notices, but God knows who we are.

Jesus Christ lived before us as the perfect example, for He was perfect. We cannot be perfect, but we can live Christlike before others. Jesus gave His life for all the world's sin. He is not asking us to die for others. He is asking us to die to self and selfish desires. There is no greater example of love than laying down your life for someone else (John 15:13). If we love others, we should live before them as Christ did. Are you living your life Christlike, or are you living for your own selfish desires?

QUESTIONS FOR REFLECTION

1. If we are evolving, why would you want to teach anything to the next generation?
2. Why would you want role models for your children to live by?
3. If everything is positive in our world, why do bad things continue to happen?

I AM THE RESURRECTION AND THE LIFE: RESTORATION

I am the resurrection and the life. He who believes in Me, though he may die, he shall live.
—JOHN 11:25

Jesus Christ walked before man to show every person how to live. He further showed man that we could know God personally. He dwelt among us, but He was not of this world. He was the perfect example in how He lived before us. However, the foundation of every Christian's belief is based upon His resurrection. When we have someone walking with us, we have a trusted friend. When we have someone living in our soul who has conquered sin, death, and the grave, we have hope—a hope that anchors the soul in every circumstance we face in life. Do you have hope in your life? What about when you die—is death the end of everything?

The Bible tells us in Ecclesiastes 3:2 that there is a time to be born and a time to die. In James 4:14, the Bible asks, "What is your life? It is even a vapor that appears for a little time and then vanishes away." I can remember something happening in my life when I was three or four years old. Though I am now seventy-six, it does not seem so long ago when that event happened. James tells us life is not really that long. Time seems to be moving faster and faster, yet the pace of time has never changed. In

Hebrews 9:27 the Bible says, "It is appointed for men to die once, but after this the judgment." We are conceived and born, we live a short time, and then we die. Solomon tells us life can be empty and meaningless if God is not part of that life. I am sure there are many people who feel their life is almost over. They are asking, "Where did it go? It seems like yesterday I was young and full of life." The cycle of life repeats itself over and over again. Is that all there is to life, a repetitive cycle?

LIFE AND DEATH

Jesus says in John 11:25–26, "I am the resurrection and the life. He who believes in Me, though he may die, he shall live. And whoever lives and believes in Me shall never die." James tells us life can be brief, like a vapor; however, Jesus tells us we can live forever. In Revelation 1:18, the Bible says, "I am He that lives and was dead, and behold I am alive forevermore." If our lives feel empty and meaningless, we can take hope in John's words in John 1:4: "In Him was life, and the life was the light of men." We can have a physical life as a descendant of our parents, but we can have a complete life through Jesus Christ.

We all have an appointment with death. There are many people who try to do everything they can to stay young. Do they fear old age and death? There are others who see no purpose in life and kill themselves. In Psalm 89:48, the Bible asks, "Can [man] deliver his life from the power of the grave?" Death is very real to us; there is no escape plan. Probably all of us know someone who has died in the last few months. There will be heartache and sorrow this side of the grave. Death is a part of everyday life. Jesus said if we believe in Him, we "will never die." Are you prepared for eternity?

God told Adam in Genesis 2:17 that if he disobeyed God, he would surely die. Many of us know people who have broken the law. How many people break the law, and it seems they are never punished? Maybe their punishment was light compared to what they did. All Adam did was disobey God's commandment. Many of the laws of man came from God's law. You may go unpunished by the judicial system in this country, but God says if you break His laws, "you will die." Disobedience is a sin to God. That sin we thought no one knew about, someone does know.

In Romans 5:12, we read that through one man, sin entered into the world and death by sin. And death was passed on to all men because all have sinned. We don't have to sin; we choose to sin. 1 John 3:4 says, "Whoever commits sin also commits lawlessness," for every sin breaks God's law. In Romans 6:23, we read, "The wages of sin is death, but the gift of God is eternal life in Jesus Christ our Lord." I am sure Adam was no different from any other person who has ever lived. He thought he could disobey God and there would not be any consequences. Breaking man's law might seem to be a little sin, and nobody will know. Man often wants to categorize his sins. God says any and all sin brings forth death. Man will also try to justify his sins by comparing himself to others. The Bible tells all of us that God is the standard, not man, and all of us have fallen short (Romans 3:23).

THERE IS A TIME

Solomon tells us there is a time to be born and a time to die. In 1 Corinthians 15:56, we read that the sting of death is sin. We sorrow in someone's death because we will miss them. There is sorrow when a believer dies, but there is also comfort in knowing that the goodbye is temporary. The Bible says to be absent from the body is to be present with the Lord (2 Corinthians 5:8). Even though everyone will experience death, it is not the end for Christians. When Jesus Christ died on the cross and rose again, the sting of sin and death ended.

The Bible says we all have an appointment with death. However, for the believer, it is just a door we will go through to enter eternity. Man will go to any means possible to stay young, for he knows he will die some-day. He will do whatever it takes to keep the outside looking young and attractive. Most people are blind to what is in the Bible when we can live forever in eternity.

People should strive to stay physically fit, but we shouldn't neglect our hearts and souls. Do you want to know how to live forever? The first step is believing the Lord Jesus Christ, repenting of your sins, and asking Christ to come into your heart.

We all have to humble ourselves before Him, or we will never see the kingdom of heaven. Whenever death comes, we will be ready and prepared to face God and eternity. God had a plan for us before we were ever created. He knew every person would sin and need redemption. From the beginning, there had to be a spotless blood sacrifice to atone for sin. Jesus Christ was the only person who met all the criteria to pay for our sins. The penalty has been paid, and eternity is our decision.

In Hebrews 9:26, we read that from the foundation of the world, Christ would come forth and suffer. By sacrificing Himself, He put away the penalty of sin. In John 10:18, Jesus said, "No one takes [my life] from Me, but I lay it down of Myself. I have power to lay it down, and I have power to take it again." From a legal standpoint, Christ was crucified unjustly. However, Christ came to earth to die. The Creator of this world and of all mankind has the power to stop anything man can do to Him. He was the first to rise from the dead, an example to all believers.

1 Corinthians 15:22 tells us, "For as in Adam all will die, even so in Christ all shall be made alive." In Romans 6:9, the Bible says that Christ is raised from the dead and will die no more; death no longer has dominion over Him.

RESURRECTED: A NEW BODY

In 1 Corinthians 15:26, we read that the last enemy that will be destroyed is death. 2 Timothy 1:10 says that Jesus Christ has abolished death and has brought life and immortality to man. You may be thinking that if Christ has abolished death, why do people continue to die? Your soul knows God's law and has free will to choose how to live. That is a choice each of us gets to make alone. In Hosea 13:14, the Bible says, "I will ransom them from the power of the grave; I will redeem them from death." Do you want to be redeemed? There is nothing more you have to do other than believe.

The Bible tells us how all believers will rise from the grave someday. Acts 24:15 says, "There shall be a resurrection of the dead, both of the just and the unjust." The Bible says the just will live with God in heaven, but the unjust will forever be in hell.

In 1 Corinthians 15, the Bible tells how Christians will be resurrected. Paul says in verses 42 through 44 that the body is sown in corruption and raised in incorruption. It is sown in dishonor and raised in glory. It is sown in weakness and raised in power. It is sown as a natural body and raised as a spiritual body. We are born in the image of man and dust, but we shall bear a heavenly image (15:49). This mortal body will not inherit heaven; a corruptible body cannot inherit an incorruptible place (15:50). Our sin-cursed body will not dwell in the same place with a holy God. When Christ calls for His people, we will all be changed from corruption to incorruption (15:51). When the trumpet is sounded, and Christ calls, the dead shall be raised incorruptible. In the twinkling of an eye, this mortal body will put on immortality (15:52–53). "O Death, where is your sting? O Hades, where is your victory?" (15:55). In 1 Thessalonians 4:16–17, we read that the Lord Himself will descend from heaven with a shout, and the dead in Christ shall rise first. Then we who are alive shall be caught up together with them in the clouds to meet the Lord. When the Rapture comes, every Christian will put on immortality. In the twinkling of the eye, we will all be changed.

Revelation 1:18 says, "I am He who lives, and was dead, and behold, I am alive forevermore. And I have the keys of Hades and of Death." In John 10:9, we read, "I am the door. If anyone enters by Me, he will be saved." God's plan is for all mankind to obtain salvation. We read in 1 Thessalonians 5:9 that God did not appoint us to wrath but to obtain salvation through our Lord Jesus Christ. In Proverbs 14:12, we read that there is a way that seems right to man, but its end is the way of death.

Adam thought there was a better way, his way. Every person gets to choose how he wants to live, but he cannot escape death.

Life and the Bible do not promise us there will be a tomorrow. But we, as Christians, have hope in the promises of Jesus Christ. The Bible tells us in Revelation 21:4 that the day is coming for believers when God will wipe away all our tears from our eyes. There shall be no more death neither sorrow, crying, or pain because the former things have passed away. Jesus says in John 14:2–3, "In My Father's house are many mansions; if it were not so, I would have told you. I go to prepare a place for you. And if I go and prepare a place for you, I will come again and receive you to Myself; that where I am, there you may be also." Jesus Christ has a prepared place for all Christians to live someday with Him. My hope is founded in my Savior and Creator. Do you have hope for tomorrow?

QUESTIONS FOR REFLECTION

1. Only Creationism presents us with eternity; do you ever think about what lies ahead when you die?
2. Do you feel you will be reincarnated and be something else when you die?
3. When you think of what comes after this life, does it bring a feeling of hope or fear?

I WILL GIVE YOU ANOTHER COMFORTER: FOREVER WITH US

And I will pray the Father, and He will give you another Helper, that He may abide with you forever.
—JOHN 14:16

The Bible says in Job 32:8 that there is a spirit in man. Every person who has ever existed has a spirit within themselves. In the second verse in the Bible, we read the Spirit of God moved upon the face of the waters. Throughout the Bible, God's presence is seen in different ways. Very early in the Bible, we see God is not "One." God is triune, three persons in one: God the Father, God the Son in Jesus Christ, and God the Holy Spirit. You may ask if the Holy Spirit is that part of God that dwells in all mankind? The answer to that question is absolutely *no*. We all have a spirit within our soul; however, the Holy Spirit is God, and His name tells us He is holy.

Jesus told Nicodemus that if he wanted to see the kingdom of God, he must be born again. If you are "born again," the Holy Spirit dwells inside your physical body. There are many people who believe in God, and some believe in Jesus Christ. What about the Holy Spirit: What do you know about Him? He is a part of God, and everyone can know Him.

It is impossible to fully describe God; how, then, can man describe the

Holy Spirit? The Bible and His presence in my soul help me to understand the Holy Spirit. He reveals God to every believer. In John 15:26, Jesus says the Holy Spirit is of God and testifies of Him. He makes God personal to each and every Christian. The Holy Spirit of God is not something that is out there somewhere; He takes residence in every believer's soul. He lives only in Christians. The Holy Spirit transcends every believer's heart and is able to live in all people and nations at the same time.

The Bible says in 1 Corinthians 12:13 that by one Spirit, all Christians are baptized into one body. All Christians have the same God and the same Spirit. We all are the same and equal in God's kingdom. Jesus tells us in John 14:26, "But the Helper, the Holy Spirit, whom the Father will send in My name, He will teach you all things, and bring to your remembrance all things that I said to you."

FREE FROM THE BONDAGE OF SIN

The Bible tells us God is Spirit. In John 4:24, we read, "God is Spirit, and those who worship Him must worship in spirit and truth." 2 Corinthians 3:17 says the Lord is the Spirit, and where the Spirit dwells, there is liberty. That liberty means where the Holy Spirit dwells, man is no longer under the bondage of sin. Because of the presence of the Holy Spirit, sin will no longer have dominion over a believer's heart and life. Sin cannot dwell in the same place at the same time with holiness.

The Holy Spirit is a person. You may be thinking, "If the Holy Spirit is a person, how can He be everywhere at the same time?" The Bible says He is a person, but it also says God is Spirit. John 14:16–17 says God "will give you another Helper, that *He* may abide with you forever—the Spirit of Truth, whom the world cannot receive because it neither sees Him nor knows Him; but you know Him" (emphasis mine). In John 16:8, we read, "And when *He* has come, *He* will convict the world of sin, and of righteousness, and of judgment" (emphasis mine). The Holy Spirit's presence in a person should manifest itself to all people. The Holy Spirit knows the voice of God and knows His ways. He is God, and true Christians reflect His nature to all the world.

ETERNAL PRESENCE

The Holy Spirit's presence was symbolized in the Bible in many ways. He is the breath of life to believers (Genesis 2:7). Exodus 3:2 chronicles Moses' first encounter with God as a burning bush. When the Jewish people left Egypt, the Spirit of God was before them as a pillar of fire by night and a pillar of cloud by day (Exodus 13:22). In Numbers 11:25, the Lord came down to Moses in a cloud and spoke with him. In Psalm 45:7, God used oil to anoint his people. In Psalm 23:5, God anointed David's head with oil. In Bible times, oil was used by religious leaders for special occasions. In Matthew 3:16, the Holy Spirit is like a dove. When Jesus was baptized and came up out of the water, immediately the heavens were opened to Him, and He saw the Spirit of God descending upon Him like a dove. Living water is also symbolized to describe the Holy Spirit. In John 4:10, Jesus tells the Samaritan woman at the well that if she knew the gift of God and asked Him, He would give her "living water." In John 7:38, Jesus says, "He who believes in Me, as the Scripture has said, out of his heart will flow rivers of living water." In Revelation 7:17, John tells us the Lamb will lead us into living fountains of water. John further tells us in Revelation 22:1 that in heaven, there is a pure river of water of life that proceeds out of the throne of God. All people who are thirsty are invited to come and drink freely of the water (22:17). Every person is invited, but only a few will choose to come.

The Holy Spirit is eternal. Psalm 90:2 says that before the mountains were brought forth, or before God formed the earth and the world, even from everlasting to everlasting, He is God. In Hebrews 9:14, we read that the blood of Christ brought the eternal Spirit when He offered Himself without spot to God. The Spirit of God has always existed, but He manifested Himself much more clearly after Christ rose from the grave.

The Holy Spirit is powerful because He is of God. After Jesus was tempted by Satan, Luke 4:14 says, "Then Jesus returned in the power of the Holy Spirit to Galilee." In Micah 3:8, we read that he is full of power by the Spirit of the Lord. Zechariah 4:6 says God is not going to do something in His strength or power but by His Spirit. Jesus tells His Apostles in Acts 1:8, "You shall receive power when the Holy Spirit has come upon you; and you shall be witnesses to Me in Jerusalem, and in all Judea and Samaria, and to the end of the earth." Jesus tells all believers in Luke 24:49, "Behold, I send the Promise of My Father upon you; but tarry in the city of Jerusalem until you are endued with power from on high."

When Jesus came to earth from heaven, it was the Holy Spirit who conceived the baby in Mary. Mary asks the angel Gabriel in Luke 1:34, "How can I be with a child for I do not know a man?" In the next verse, Gabriel tells her the Holy Spirit will come upon her, and the power of God will overtake her. The baby born of her would be holy. In Matthew 1:20, the Bible says, "That which is conceived in her is of the Holy Spirit." If Jesus had been conceived by Mary and Joseph, He would have had the sin nature of all mankind. He would not have been the perfect, sinless sacrifice required for the atonement of man's sins.

Genesis 1:2 says, "And the Spirit of God was hovering over the face of the waters." The Bible says in Psalm 104:24, "O Lord, how manifold are Your works! In wisdom You have made them all. The earth is full of Your possessions." In verse 30, we read, "You send forth Your Spirit, they are created; and You renew the face of the earth." Everything that exists in our universe reveals a master Creator.

Believers know the truth, for it dwells within us. In John 16:13, Jesus says, "When He, the Spirit of truth, has come, He will guide you into all truth; for He will not speak on His own *authority,* but whatever He hears He will speak; and He will tell you things to come." Absolute truth can be known, for it is of God. Being politically correct is man's way of justifying his actions, twisting the truth into something that satisfies his sinful nature. Because God is true, the Holy Spirit will guide you in all truth.

THE WIND

Jesus tells us in John 3:8, "The wind blows where it wishes, and you hear the sound of it, but you cannot tell where it comes from and where it goes. So is everyone who is born of the Spirit." Every person feels the wind blow. How is it that some people have the Holy Spirit and others do not? All creation reveals God to all mankind. God is Spirit, and He is everywhere. He is trying to reveal Himself to every person. Do you feel the wind? David tells us in Psalm 38:4, "For my iniquities have gone over my head; like a heavy burden they are too heavy for me." The Holy Spirit of God makes known to us our sins and reveals them to our souls.

Man will never see himself unless the Holy Spirit shows him who he really is. The Bible says in 1 Corinthians 2:14 that the natural man does not receive the things of the Spirit of God, for they are foolishness to him, nor can he know them. Jesus tells us in John 6:44, "No one can come to Me unless the Father who sent Me draws him." God always reaches down to man first; it is not in man's nature to reach out to God. To be drawn toward something is to draw or pull toward it, to cause something to move or go forth.[37] The Holy Spirit reveals sin in your life, and when sin is revealed, it pulls on your heartstrings. In John 16:8, Jesus says, "And when He (the Holy Spirit) has come, He will convict the world of sin, and of righteousness, and of judgment" (parenthetical mine). To convict means to find fault with sin. The Spirit of God is around every person. Hearts that are receptive to God will see their sin nature and will become convicted of those sins.

Jesus said in John 6:63, "It is the Spirit who gives life; the flesh profits nothing. The words that I speak to you are spirit, and they are life." When you receive the Holy Spirit, He will make you come alive or show forth life. The Holy Spirit reveals sin to man because all mankind sins. He convicts you and finds fault with your lifestyle. He draws you to God and leads you to godly repentance; He quickens your heart. Your old sin

---

[37] "Draw," *American Heritage Dictionary of the English Language.*

nature and your burdens are washed white as snow with the blood of Jesus Christ. From that point, the Holy Spirit is no longer around you; He dwells within your heart and soul forevermore. However, the Holy Spirit cannot live within you until you ask God to come into your heart. Romans 8:11 says that the same Spirit that raised Jesus from the dead is the Spirit that dwells in Christians. If you are not a Christian, wherever you go, the wind will blow. You cannot escape from it; God is trying to reach your heart. Do you still feel the wind?

The Holy Spirit reveals to believers what they need to know to go forth throughout life. The presence of the Holy Spirit is immediate when we ask Christ to come into our hearts. Psalm 37:23 says the steps of a good man are ordered by the Lord, and he delights in walking His way. What happens in man's heart when the Holy Spirit dwells there? In Ezekiel 36:27, we read, "I will put My Spirit within you and cause you to walk in My statutes, and you will keep My judgments." If we walk in the Spirit, He will direct our steps. Jesus tells us in John 14:26 that the Holy Spirit will teach us all things and bring to our memory all things He has said. In 1 Corinthians 2:13, the Bible says we are to speak as the Holy Spirit teaches us, discerning all things. 1 John 2:27 says the anointing that we have received from God will teach us all things in truth because there is no lie in truth. When the Holy Spirit dwells in us, He will manifest the character of God to our souls. The living God takes residence inside our hearts. The Holy Spirit will guide us to be more Christlike and less like sinful man.

Life will present problems to every person, and Christians are just as susceptible to them as unbelievers. However, help is always present when God dwells inside our hearts. Isaiah 41:10 tells us to "fear not, for I am with you; be not dismayed for I am your God. I will strengthen you, yes, I will help you." In 2 Corinthians 5:7, Christians are told to walk by faith, not by sight. The Holy Spirit will direct every step we take in life.

The Holy Spirit is a living person who dwells inside every believer. He is there to teach, guide, help, and comfort Christians as we go through life.

We have a constant companion. In Hebrews 13:5, the Bible says, "I will never leave you nor forsake you." Knowing God is with you wherever you go, whatever the circumstances, brings comfort and peace to this mortal soul. Is there anyone in your life for whom you can say he will never leave you or forsake you?

FREE WILL

The Holy Spirit does not control any person. He is not some mind-altering force that takes control of your body. The free will God placed in your soul will be there as long as you live. Being a Christian does not remove your free will. God will not force you to obey Him. Each of us determines how much of God we allow into our heart. The Holy Spirit will never do anything to harm you. He will always direct you toward God, His truth, and His righteousness. God always wants us to seek Him and His way. In Him is where we find real life.

Even though the Holy Spirit dwells in every Christian, they don't always live as they should. Man can quench, suppress, or grieve the Holy Spirit. That which indwells believers lives and is holy by His nature. True Christians should manifest the character of Christ. However, every person can become weighted down by the circumstances of life. Then, too, there are people who claim to be Christians when they are not. The true Holy Spirit of God wants to manifest Himself to the world. In 1 Corinthians 3:16–17, we read that we are the temple of God, and the Spirit of God lives in us. The temple of God is holy. Which temple are you, the one that exalts and worships self or the one who exalts and worships God?

Do you have any fear of God? The Bible warns people about how they are to approach God. In Matthew 12:31, the Bible says, "Every sin and blasphemy will be forgiven men, but the blasphemy against the Spirit will not be forgiven men." *The Pictorial Bible Dictionary* defines blasphemy as cursing God and the Holy Spirit. *The American Heritage Dictionary of the English Language* says it is profane speaking about God. When Jesus speaks in Matthew 12, He does not say, "If you blasphemed Me, you would not be forgiven." Why would Jesus say we can blaspheme Him but not the Holy Spirit? I believe the reason is that the Holy Spirit reveals sin to man; He convicts us of our sins; He draws us to Jesus Christ, and He quickens or changes our hearts, and we become "born again."

The Holy Spirit will always testify of Jesus Christ. In John 16:14, Jesus says, "He (the Holy Spirit) will glorify Me, for He will take what is Mine and declare it to you" (parenthetical mine). Jesus tells us in John 14:26, "The Helper, the Holy Spirit, whom the Father will send in My name, He will teach you all things." Amazement is an understatement to try and explain how or why God would dwell in my mortal body. I have a small part of God's presence within me because there was a time when a thirteen-year-old boy asked Jesus Christ to come into his heart.

Are you intrigued about the future? In John 16:13, we read that the Holy Spirit will guide us into all truth and it will show us things to come. I believe one of the greatest things I have learned from reading through the Bible is that I can see the world with clear, unobstructed sight. 1 Timothy 4:1 says, "The Spirit expressly says that in latter times some will depart from the faith, giving heed to deceiving spirits and doctrines of demons." I believe we are now living in the latter times. The Bible and the Holy Spirit reveal absolute truth and perfect vision to see what is happening in the world. The question is not are we in the latter days; rather, the question is when is Christ coming to rapture His church? Are you ready for Christ to come again? If you are not a Christian, can you still feel the wind around you? The Holy Spirit lives, and He can give you life—a life you have never had before and a life that is eternal.

QUESTIONS FOR REFLECTION

1. With Creationism, we have the capability of a direct connection to God. With other theories of the origin of life, do you have a connection with anyone?

2. Is there anything in your heart that you can hold onto as you go through life?

3. What brings comfort and peace to you?

IN THE BEGINNING WAS THE WORD: COMPASS AND GUIDE

In the beginning was the Word, and the Word
was with God, and the Word was God.
—JOHN 1:1

What comes to your mind when you hear or think of the Bible? Whether you have little knowledge or understanding of the Bible, its truths and principles are incredibly relevant to you and to the time we live in today. "In God we trust" is on the money we use every day in our lives. In the courtroom, the Bible is used when a person swears to tell the truth. Furthermore, the Bible is used when someone is sworn into public office. God's presence is manifested in our culture and lives wherever we go in America. What about the Bible—is it just a book to lay on the bookshelf and collect dust?

There is basic information about the Bible, and there is the substance of it, God's Word. The Bible is a collection of sixty-six separate books that are incomplete of themselves. Most Bibles have sixty-six books, and some religions use Bibles that have more books. God's plan and purpose are continuous throughout all the books. Therefore, each book does not present the complete story. Christians recognize the Bible as God's inspired Word revealing Himself and His will to mankind. The Bible is divided into the Old Testament, consisting of thirty-nine books, and the New Testament, containing twenty-seven books. It was written over approximately 1600 years by many different authors. My study Bible says there were twenty-two writers, and some sources say there were up to forty-four writers. No one source of information knows for sure who wrote some of the books. We do know there were many writers over time, and very few knew each other. Yet the Bible is one continuous story of God's plan for all mankind.

GOD'S WORD IS STEADFAST AND TRUE

The central focus of the Bible is Jesus Christ. Although He is not specifically called by name in the Old Testament, He has always existed. To Bible scholars, His presence is seen very clearly in the Old Testament. From the foundations of the world, God had a plan to redeem man from the penalty of sin and death. That plan is written for everyone to see in the Bible—one book about one God and one way for all mankind to see the kingdom of heaven.

The Bible has all the answers to life. You might ask, "If it has all the answers, why can't I understand what it says?" By God's grace and mercy, all people can understand a little of the Bible. The Bible says in Titus 2:11, "The grace of God that brings salvation has appeared to all men." Every person can understand enough of the Bible to be saved. It is that simple and complete for anyone to understand. You will not be able to grasp the deeper things of the Bible until you are a Christian. The Holy Spirit of God will reveal things to you as you grow as a believer. The Bible is inspired by God, and when you have the Holy Spirit in you, you will better understand what it says. Mortal man will never fully understand the Bible because we don't have the mind of Christ. We won't truly see God or know Him unless we are a Christian. So if we cannot understand the Bible, is it true? What can we learn from it?

The Bible says in John 1:1, "In the beginning was the Word, and the Word was with God, and the Word was God." When did the beginning start? The Bible says the Word existed with God before anything was created. If you believe in God, the Bible says, "The Word was God." We read in Psalm 119:89, "Forever, O Lord, Your word is settled in heaven." Isaiah 40:8 says, "The grass withers, the flower fades, but the Word of our God stands forever." In Psalm 119:160, the Bible says that every Word of God is truth and endures forever.

We hold onto God's promises because of what we believe about God and the Bible. Forever, O Lord, your word is settled in heaven and to all mankind, for it is true because you are true. If God is not true, there is no standard to go by to determine what is true. We read in Psalm 33:4, "The word of the Lord is right, and all His work is done in truth." Psalm 100:5 says, "The Lord is good; His mercy is everlasting, and His truth endures to all generations." There is a standard for truth, and it has always existed. Because God is true, the Bible is true. Being politically correct is just another way of lying.

There are other verses that state the Bible has existed from the beginning and will last forever. In Matthew 24:35, we read, "Heaven and earth will pass away, but My words will by no means pass away." Peter tells us in 1 Peter 1:25, "'But the word of the Lord endures forever.' Now this is the word which by the gospel was preached to you." In 1 John 1:1, the Bible says, "That which was from the beginning. which we have heard, which we have seen with our eyes, which we have looked upon, and our hands have handled, concerning the Word of life." Scripture tells us very plainly: The Bible is the Word of God.

GOD'S WORD IS INSPIRED BY HIM

Man will tell you he believes in God, but the Bible is irrelevant. He may also ask, "If the Bible has always existed, why was it written by man?" Even though the Bible was written by man, it was divinely inspired by God. In 2 Peter 1:21, we read, "For prophecy never came by the will of man, but holy men of God spoke as they were moved by the Holy Spirit." Although man printed the Bible as we see it now, God wrote it. John 1:14 says,

"The Word was made flesh and dwelt among us." God became flesh and blood in Jesus Christ. He revealed Himself to everyone He encountered. In Romans 7:12, we see that the law is holy, and the commandments are holy, just, and good. Because God is holy, every Word of God is holy. If man had written the Bible, it could not be holy. Man put the Bible in print as he was directed by God. In Revelation 19:13, we read that when Christ returns to earth, He will be clothed with a robe dipped in blood, and His name is called "The Word of God."

Man will seek God when trouble arises in his life, not knowing the presence of God lies on a shelf untouched and unread. The Bible states God, Jesus Christ, and the Bible are the same. The plan of God is complete in the Bible; the road map is in our homes.

In Psalm 147:15, we read that God sent his commandments to earth. In Romans 16:26 we see that the scriptures were given by the prophets and were made known to all nations. God wrote the Ten Commandments and gave them to Moses in (Exodus 20:1–17). Those commandments instructed man in how he was to live before God and before other people. The first four commandments relate to our relationship with God. The last six commandments tell us how we are to live with other people. You may say you don't have to obey God's laws. In Romans 2:14–15, the Bible says that when you do something by nature, things contained in a law, then what you do are laws to you. Civilized man lives by a set of laws, whether from God or from the society in which he lives. Every one of us has some set of rules we live by. A Pharisee lawyer asked Jesus, "What is the greatest commandment?" Jesus told him in Matthew 22:35–39, "'You shall love the Lord your God with all your heart, with all your soul, and with all your mind.' This is the first and great commandment. And the second is like it: 'You shall love your neighbor as yourself.'" Jesus told him if he obeyed those two commandments, he would be obedient to any and every law God would ask him to do. Laws are given to man to guide and protect him. They can direct us in life and place boundaries on what is acceptable behavior. The Bible contains all of God's law.

GOD'S WORD IS PURPOSEFUL, POWERFUL, PERFECT, AND PURE

Although the Bible was written by Jewish people, it is applicable to everyone. Every person was created by God and has the same basic needs. The Holy Spirit does not discriminate against any person; neither does the Bible. In Isaiah 55:11, the Bible says that God's Word will go forth and not return void, and it will accomplish that which pleases Him and will prosper wherever He sends it. Every one of God's purposes will come to pass.

There is probably no greater verse in the Bible to fully describe how powerful God's Word is than Hebrews 4:12: "For the word of God is living and powerful, and sharper than any two-edged sword, piercing even to the division of soul and spirit, and of joints and marrow, and is a discerner of the thoughts and intents of the heart." The reason the Bible is able to do all these things is because the Word is "God." Only God knows everything about us, even our thoughts.

The Bible says in 2 Samuel 22:31 that God's way is perfect, for the word of the Lord is proven, and He will protect all who trust in Him. In Psalm 19:7, we read, "The law of the Lord is perfect, converting the soul; the testimony of the Lord is sure, making wise the simple." The Bible is able to make someone uneducated wise because it is God who gives us true wisdom. Truth will set you free from a load that is often too heavy to carry because of the guilt that is associated with living a lie.

Another word that describes the Bible is pure. For something to be pure, it cannot be mixed with anything; it is complete, authentic, perfect, and without fault. The Bible says in Psalm 12:6 that the words of the Lord are pure as silver tried in a furnace and purified seven times. In Psalm 19:8, we read that the commandments of the Lord are pure, enlightening the eyes. In Proverbs 30:5, we see that every word of God is pure, and He is a shield to everyone who puts their trust in Him. If you read the Bible, you will hold in your hands truth, light, and purity. The one and only God who created us manifests these characteristics within Himself, and they are expressed in His Word, the Bible.

GOD'S WORD IS SEED AND LIGHT

Jesus tells us in Mark 4:3–20 and Luke 8:5–15 that the Bible is like a seed. Every person who reads it will respond to it differently. God's Word is sown as seed. Some of it will be trampled on the ground, and some of it will lodge in hard places and cannot take root. Some of it will lodge in man's heart, but the cares of the world will keep it from growing. But there are some people in whom the Word takes root and bears much fruit. This pattern is the same in every person. We all will choose how we respond to God and the Bible. In 2 Corinthians 9:10, we read that God gives us seed, and it is bread for food, and the fruit of those seeds will help us grow in righteousness. Jesus tells us in John 5:24, "He who hears My word and believes in Him who sent Me has everlasting life, and shall not come into judgment, but has passed from death into life."

In Deuteronomy 8:2–3, the Bible tells the Jewish people to remember how the Lord led them out of Egypt. They suffered hunger and thirst, and God fed them with manna from heaven that none of their fathers knew. God fed them that they may know man does not live by bread alone, but by every word that proceeds out of the mouth of the Lord. In Psalm 119:103, we read that the Word of God is sweeter than honey to taste. The Bible becomes more desirable the more you read it!

The Bible is more than just food for the soul; in Micah 2:7, we read that the Word of God will cause us to walk in the right way. Jesus tells us in John 15:3 that we can be clean through His Word. In Psalm 107:20, we read that His Word will heal and deliver us from destruction. Psalm 119:165 says, "Great peace have those who love Your law." In every area of our lives, God's Word can help us.

God told Moses in Deuteronomy 6:7–9 that we are to have His Word with us everywhere we go. I have a Bible on my phone, one in my car, a study Bible at home, and another one I use when I go to church. The Christian's greatest defense and help in the world is in God and the Bible. Joshua 1:8 says, "This book of the law shall not depart from your mouth, but you shall meditate in it day and night, that you may observe to do according to all that is written in it." If we meditate on something, it is at the forefront of our minds. An idle mind, on the contrary, is a playground for the devil to entice and deceive you.

In Galatians 6:7, we read that whatsoever a man sows, that he will also reap. In Isaiah 5:24, the Bible says, "They have rejected the law of the LORD of hosts, and despised the word of the Holy One of Israel." In 2 Thessalonians 2:3, we read, "Let no one deceive you by any means; for that Day will not come unless the falling away comes first, and the man of sin is revealed." When that happens, men will no longer know what is true. Are we living in that day? The Bible tells us in Romans 7:7 that we did not know what sin was until we read God's Word. In Numbers 32:23, we read that our sins will find us. Man knows he sins. The Bible says in Isaiah 5:24, "As the fire devours the stubble, and the flame consumes the chaff, so their root will be as rottenness, and their blossom will ascend like dust; because they have rejected the law of the LORD." Eternal life and eternal death can be found in God's Word. Solomon tells us in Proverbs 30:6 that if we change God's Words, He will rebuke us and we will be found a liar. The Bible tells us exactly who we are.

Another word that expressly defines God and the Bible is light. In Psalm 43:3, we read, "Send Your light and Your truth! Let them lead me." If you live your life in truth, you will be in the light of God. He created light first. Genesis 1:2–5 says the earth was without form and void, and darkness was upon the face of the deep. Then God said, "Let there be light," and there was light. God divided the light from the darkness and called the light day and the darkness night. In John 1:4–5, we read that Christ is the life and light of men. Man, however, does not want to live in truth, nor does he want to walk in the light. In 2 Peter 1:19, we read that the Word of God shines in dark places. In Psalm 119:105, we see that the Bible is a lamp unto our feet and a light unto our path. Similarly, Psalm 119:130 says that reading God's Word gives light and understanding to the simple. God created light so that man would not stumble in the dark.

Furthermore, light exposes everything about man's sin nature. In Psalm 139:12, we read that the darkness and the light are the same to God.

The Bible shines light on the sinful nature of man. In Romans 15:4, we read, "For whatever things were written before were written for our learning, that we through the patience and comfort of the Scriptures might have hope." 1 Corinthians 10:11 says, "Now all these things happened to them as examples, and they were written for our admonition." The Bible presents to us both sides of every situation. There is God's way, and there is man's way. Because it is embedded in every person's soul, they all know there is a God. A missionary from Africa came to my church and said the native people in the deepest part of that country knew there was a God.

The Bible says in Psalm 19:7–8, "The law of the Lord is perfect, converting the soul; the testimony of the LORD is sure, making wise the simple; the statutes of the LORD are right, rejoicing the heart; the commandment of the LORD is pure, enlightening the eyes." Furthermore, because God lives, the Bible lives. Regardless of the number of times you read the Bible, you will read a verse, and it will speak to you differently than ever before. Every Christian who reads his Bible will tell you the meaning of a verse can change over time. The Bible lives because it was written by the living God. In Esther 4:14, we read, "For such a time as this." God knows our needs, and He knows the exact time in which we need His presence. The Bible is filled with verses showing God's provision "for such a time is this."

The Bible has all we need for life and eternity. However, the Bible is a two-edged sword that can give life and also take it. It is a guide that will direct all our steps with warning signs. If we were traveling down a road and a sign said, "Bridge out ahead," would we ignore that sign? Life and death are presented for us in the Bible. Read on if you want to know more.

GOD'S WORD TELLS US WHAT IS TO COME

There is another part of the Bible that deals with the life we live here on earth. The Bible tells us in Isaiah 64:4, "For since the beginning of the world men have not heard nor perceived by the ear, nor has the eye seen any God besides You, who acts for the one who waits for Him." You may think the Bible is nothing more than a book of laws telling you things you can and cannot do. The Bible tells *me* there is joy and life ever after by following God. Do you want to know what the Bible says about you and me? The Bible gives us examples of how all people have lived before. It tells us the good and bad of man; it gives directions on how to live, and it gives us warning about the dangers of the road we may be traveling. Furthermore, it tells us that someday, we will stand before a judge. The Bible does not leave anything out; everything we need to know in life can be found in it. Do you want to know why you may face a judge someday?

I said earlier that in the latter days, man will not know what is true. The disciples came to Jesus and asked Him when that time would be. Jesus tells us one of the signs in Matthew 24:14: "This gospel of the kingdom will be preached in all the world as a witness to all the nations, and then the end will come." In Romans 10:18, we read, "Have they not heard? Yes indeed: 'Their sound has gone out to all the earth, and their words to the ends of the world.'" In Romans 16:26, the Bible says that the Scriptures have gone out by the prophets to all nations according to the commandment of the everlasting God. Satellites, the internet, television, and radio are now able to spread the Bible all over the world. By God's design, there is no place man can go that He is not already there. He has made a way for you to know how to find Him.

Warning signs are throughout the Bible. We get to choose whether to obey them or not. If we do not heed the warnings, judgment day is coming. The Bible tells us in Deuteronomy 32:4 that God's work is perfect and that He is a God of truth and justice. All His ways are just and righteous, as He is just and righteous.

Maybe part of the reason man does not fear judgment is because of our laws in this country. Solomon tells us in Ecclesiastes 8:11, "Because the sentence against an evil work is not executed speedily, therefore the heart of the sons of men is fully set in them to do evil." Proverbs 28:5 says, "Evil men do not understand justice, but those who seek the Lord understand all."

Whether you believe in man's way of doing things or God's, every person will die someday. The Bible says in Hebrews 9:27 that it is appointed for men to die once, but after this is the judgment. Death is coming—are you prepared? You may escape justice with man, but you will not with God. Romans 2:16 tells us God will judge the secrets of men by Jesus Christ. With God, there are no secrets, and there are no places you can hide.

The Bible is relevant and is as up-to-date as any book on human behavior. When a person writes about human behavior, he thinks that is the way man acts. His opinions are based upon his education and what he has been taught. God created man, and He knows exactly his character. Ecclesiastes 1:9 says there is no new thing under the sun. You may think things are different now, but the Bible says men have never changed. Man just wraps up sin in a different box and presents it differently. Man does not have any excuses. In 2 Timothy 3:15, the Bible says, "From childhood you have known the Holy Scriptures, which are able to make you wise for salvation." Every person knows about the Bible. It is filled with examples, directions, and warnings. It can direct you through every step in life. With something that important, do you want to leave it on the shelf and collect dust?

QUESTIONS FOR REFLECTION

1. Do you have a source for absolute truth? How does the idea that "the truth will set you free" resonate with you?
2. Where (or to whom) do you go for wise counsel or guidance in your life?
3. Does your source for guidance present both sides of the situation, the good and the bad?

DOES THE DEVIL REALLY EXIST? WHAT ABOUT ANGELS: TEMPTATION AND DECEPTION

For by Him all things were created that are in heaven and that are on earth, visible and invisible, whether thrones or dominions or principalities or powers.
—COLOSSIANS 1:16

Creation involves more than man and the world in which he lives. What about other beings—do they exist? The Bible says there are angels among us. What do you know about angels? We read in Psalm 148:2–5, "Praise Him, all His angels; praise Him, all His hosts! Praise Him, sun and moon; praise Him, all you stars of light! Praise Him, you heavens of heavens, and you waters above the heavens! Let them praise the name of the LORD, for He commanded and they were created." In Colossians 1:16, we read, "For by Him all things were created that are in heaven and that are on earth, visible and invisible, whether thrones or dominions or principalities or powers. All things were created through Him and for Him."

In Genesis 3:24, God sets cherubim at the entrance to the Garden of Eden to prevent man from entering in. Genesis 16:71 says the Angel of the

LORD found Hagar in the wilderness. Sarah, Abraham's wife, had forced Hagar to leave her home after she conceived his son Ishmael. Hagar was a maid or concubine in the home of Abraham. In Genesis 22:11–12, we see that the Angel of the LORD stopped Abraham from sacrificing his son Isaac on the altar. The Bible tells us in Hebrews 1:14 that angels are ministering spirits sent forth to believers. We do not know how many angels there are because the Bible does not tell us. In Revelation 5:11, John heard the voice of many angels around the throne of God, and the number of them was ten thousand times ten thousand and thousands of thousands. If you multiply all those thousands, you should get about 100 trillion. That is a lot of angels around us, considering we cannot see them! They are ministering spirits sent by God to fulfill His plans and purposes.

ANGELS INVISIBLE, BUT AMONG US

There is not a lot written about angels in the Bible. They are always used to show God and His will to man. In every situation, they are doing something for God. They are not all-knowing; only God is all-knowing. In Matthew 24:36, we read that angels do not know the time when Christ will come back to earth again. Luke 20:34–36 tells us angels do not marry. We read in Psalm 103:20 that angels excel in strength because they do what is needed for God. We find in Psalm 8:5 that angels were created higher than man. Even though angels are created higher than man, 1 Corinthians 6:3 tells us the saints of God will judge angels in heaven. In Jude 9 we find there is some distinction or classes of angels. Michael is an archangel, and he is the only angel in the Bible titled an archangel. Another angel stated by name is Gabriel, who was sent forth to proclaim the news to Mary that she would conceive and bear Jesus Christ. He is also written about prophetically in Daniel 8:15–27.

Matthew 18:10 tells us angels watch over little children. If angels are watching our kids, that should tell us how important children are to God. We should love our children, not abuse or abort them. After Jesus was tempted by Satan, angels came to minister to Him (Matthew 4:11).

In Luke 22:43, Jesus was burdened about going to the cross and being crucified. Angels came and ministered to Him then as well. In Matthew 28:2–7, the Bible says angels rolled the stone away from the tomb where Christ had been buried. Further, in Acts 1:10–11, angels were present when Jesus ascended to heaven.

We know angels are supernatural in all they do. Although they do not have a physical body, they are personified as beings. They are not glorified humans, and they are very distinct from man. Although they are supernatural in almost every way, they cannot control the will of men.[38] Every person has free will to choose how he wants to live. An angel's power is submissive to what God allows them to do. Angels cannot manipulate the minds of men. In every area of your life, you choose what you want to do.

THE SERPENT, SATAN, AND THE DEVIL

Angels are like humans in that they have a free will. They are not forced to love and obey God. They, too, were created. However, one-third of the angels were thrown out of heaven. If we go back to the beginning, the first mention of an angel is in Genesis 3:1, when God set cherubim to guard the entrance to the Garden of Eden. In Revelation 12:9, the Bible says, "The serpent of old, called the Devil and Satan, who deceives the whole world; he was cast to the earth, and his angels were cast out with him." Jesus tells us in Luke 10:18, "I saw Satan fall like lightning from heaven." You may not know, but Satan, at one time, was with God in heaven. How could an angel created by God be cast out of heaven? What happened that something created to glorify God could become so different from how he was created? In Isaiah 43:7, the Bible tells us all men were created to glorify God. What has happened to man?

There are two books in the Bible that tell us about the nature of Satan. Bible scholars do not totally agree these verses apply to Satan's character; however, I feel they describe Satan very well and tell us why God cast him

---

[38] "Angels," *Pictorial Bible Dictionary.*

out of heaven. Furthermore, what Satan did in heaven is characteristic of the nature of mankind. The Bible tells us in Isaiah 14:12–15, "How you are fallen from heaven, O Lucifer, son of the morning! How you are cut down to the ground, you who weakened the nations! For you have said in your heart: 'I will ascend into heaven, I will exalt my throne above the stars of God; I will also sit on the mount of the congregation on the farthest sides of the north; I will ascend above the heights of the clouds, I will be like the Most High.' Yet you shall be brought down to Sheol." Satan made himself equal to or better than God. He was a created being, yet he decided he would be god. Jesus tells us in Matthew 23:12, "And whoever exalts himself will be humbled, and he who humbles himself will be exalted." If we exalt ourselves, we will fall.

In Ezekiel 27:3, we read that Satan said, "I am perfect in beauty." God tells Satan in Ezekiel 28:1–8:

> *"Because your heart is lifted up, and you say, 'I am a god, I sit in the seats of gods, in the midst of seas,' yet you are a man, and not a god, though you set your heart as the heart of a god . . . therefore thus says the LORD God: "Because you have set your heart as the heart of a god . . . they shall throw you down into the Pit."*

In verse 13, we read that he was in the Garden of Eden, and verse 14 says he was on the holy mountain of God. Verse 15 says he was perfect in his ways from the day he was created until iniquity was found in him, and verse 17 reads, "Your heart was lifted up because of your beauty; you corrupted your wisdom for the sake of your splendor." God cast him to the ground.

Jesus tells us in Mark 7:21–22 that from within the heart comes evil thoughts. Solomon tells us in Proverbs 16:18 that pride goes before destruction. Anytime man lifts his heart up to God, he better be looking for a soft spot to land because he will fall. We read in 1 Timothy 3:6 that if we are puffed up with pride, we will fall like Satan fell. Satan was created perfect;

he may have been the most beautiful angel in heaven. But he wanted to be God even though he was created by Him.

When Satan was cast out of heaven, he took one-third of the stars in heaven with him (Revelation 12:4). One-third of the angels God created were cast down to earth. God has ministering spirits to fulfill His will to all believers, but Satan has demons that help him do his will. His demons try to keep you from being saved and hinder a believer's testimony to others.

What does the Bible tell us about Satan and his character? Job 1:12 tells us Satan's power is limited. Satan could take everything from Job but his life. In Matthew 4:3, we read how Satan tempted Jesus by offering Him everything. But Satan was no match for Christ. In James 1:13, the Bible says, "God cannot be tempted by evil, nor does He Himself tempt anyone." Satan also tempted Judas to betray Christ with thirty pieces of silver.

Matthew 13:19 tells us that when someone reads the Bible, Satan will hinder their ability to understand what they are reading. God's Word will be sown; however, Satan will try to keep a person from responding to it. The Bible tells us in 1 Corinthians 10:20 to not have fellowship with demons. Too many times, man would rather walk in the dark of sin rather than in the light. Satan will try to keep us in the dark, but there is light if only we will look.

Satan is described in many ways in the Bible. When first noted in the Bible, he is a serpent (Genesis 3:1). The serpent deceived Adam and Eve in the Garden of Eden. In John 8:44, Jesus tells the Pharisees, "You are of your father the devil, and the desires of your father you want to do. He was a murderer from the beginning, and does not stand in the truth, because there is no truth in him. When he speaks a lie he speaks from his own resources, for he is a liar and the father of it." In 2 Thessalonians 2:9–10, we read that Satan lies and uses deception to keep people from knowing the truth. John tells us in Revelation 12:9, "The serpent of old, called the Devil and Satan who deceives the whole world; he was cast to the earth, and his angels were cast out with him."

The Bible says in 2 Corinthians 11:13–14 that some religious leaders are false and deceiving people. We should not be surprised Satan has people working for him because he transformed himself into an angel of light. If we do not know what is true, we cannot see truth or light. In 2 Corinthians 11:3–4, we read that the serpent deceived Eve through his craftiness. Coming to know Jesus Christ is very simple, but Satan makes everyone believe it is difficult. Satan, the god of this world, has blinded the minds of those who do not believe. In 2 Thessalonians 2:2, Paul writes that the day of Christ is at hand, and we should not be shaken in mind, troubled, or deceived. If we are not grounded in truth, we are vulnerable to Satan's tactics and deception.

We are warned in 1 John 3:8 that he who commits sin is of the devil, for the devil sinned from the beginning. Every person will sin; however, if we continue to sin, we are of the devil. In 1 John 5:19, we read that the whole world lies under the influence of the wicked one. Satan hates God and goodness. He wants to destroy God's plan for man by deceiving every person into sinning and doing evil. He has one-third of the created angels working for him; therefore, he is not alone in trying to deceive man.

Satan has many names in the Bible, and you may not be familiar with some of them. 1 Peter 5:8 says, "Be sober, be vigilant, because your adversary the devil walks about like a roaring lion, seeking whom he may devour." An adversary is an opponent or enemy.[39] In Revelation 9:11, Satan is called Abaddon or Apollyon. According to *The Bible Pictorial Dictionary,* Abaddon is ruin and destruction; it is the home of the dead. Apollyon is the name for the prince of darkness. In Revelation 12:10, Satan is called the accuser of the brethren. An accuser brings charges against you. In Matthew 12:24, he is called Beelzebub, "the ruler of all demons." Ephesians 2:2 calls him the prince of the power of the air. He is very powerful, but only God is all-powerful. In 1 Thessalonians 3:5, he is called the tempter. A tempter is someone who entices, seduces, invites, or provokes you to do something unwise or immoral. All these titles reflect ways in which all men are drawn away from God's commandments of how we are to live. God did not cre-

---

[39] "Adversary," *The American Heritage Dictionary of the English Language.*

ate sin; man chooses to sin. Adam and Eve were deceived by the serpent; however, they chose to disobey God.

John 12:31 tells us, "Now is the judgment of this world; now the ruler of this world will be cast out." John tells us in Revelation 12:12 that we are to rejoice because Satan knows he only has a short time to live on earth. In Matthew 8:28–29, Jesus met two people who were possessed with devils. The demons knew Christ was the Son of God. They asked Jesus, "Have You come here to torment us before the time?" Satan and his angels know their time is limited. Because Jesus Christ voluntarily went to the cross and became the blood sacrifice for every person's sin, the ultimate power of Satan is defeated. He has a short time to deceive the world.

The Bible tells us Satan and his demons seek whomever they can devour. If you are not a Christian, you do not have the absolute truth dwelling within your heart and soul. That adversary, that roaring lion, is around you and desires to control you. There is a bright light shining through the darkness to guide you to Jesus Christ; if only you will look, you will find Him.

Ephesians 6:12 says, "For we do not wrestle against flesh and blood, but against principalities, against powers, against the rulers of the darkness of this age, against spiritual hosts of wickedness in the heavenly places." God wants you to know the truth, but Satan will lie to you. Furthermore, he is a murderer and will deceive you into making sin look appealing to you. The apostle Paul tells us in 1 Corinthians 14:33, "For God is not the author of confusion but of peace." Are you confused? Has this world's philosophy blinded you to the point where you no longer know what to believe? The power of Satan and death no longer have control over man because Jesus Christ has broken the chains of bondage to sin. There are angels among us. Are they guiding you toward truth and light or darkness and sin?

QUESTIONS FOR REFLECTION

1. Have you ever felt there was someone near you, but you could not see anyone?

2. Have you ever felt as though someone or something was trying to control your mind?

3. Does the unknown create fear in your heart?

WHO IS MAN? THE HEART AND FLESH OF MAN

What is man that You are mindful of him, and
the son of man that You visit him?
—PSALM 8:4

W hat do you know about the heart and soul of man? Should we be more alike if we evolved? In every area of life—physically, mentally, and emotionally—each person is a unique creation by God. The Bible tells us man is fearfully and wonderfully made (Psalm 139:14). God, Jesus Christ, and the Holy Spirit together formed man. Every person came about by design, and we have a part of God's likeness in us.

Psalm 8:4-5 says, "What is man that You are mindful of him, and the son of man that You visit him? For You have made him a little lower than the angels, and You have crowned him with glory and honor." In verse 6, we read that God made man to have dominion over all His creation and put all things under his feet. I believe when God formed Adam and Eve from the dust of the ground, they were made perfect. There was no sin. There was God, Adam and Eve, and a perfect world in which to live. Can you envision a perfect physical body, a heart and soul without sin, and a perfect world in which to live? That was the way God designed it to be for Adam and Eve. With so much going on in the world today, we can only imagine how it could have been. When the serpent (Satan) appeared in Genesis 3, however, everything changed. How could it have happened so quickly? I believe nothing has changed in the heart of man since creation. It is time to get out a mirror and take a good look at yourself.

When we go back to the beginning, the fall of man took place within the first three chapters of the Bible. Psalm 16:6 says we have a good heritage. Paul tells us in 1 Timothy 4:4 that every creature of God is good. Furthermore, we read in Malachi 2:15 that there is only one godly seed. Isaiah 45:13 says God raised us up in righteousness. Adam and Eve were created from perfect seed. What happened that led them on a spiraling road where they could no longer control their own destiny?

Every person has a soul with a moral conscience. Adam was created God-focused, but he saw something he thought would make him better. He was instructed by God how he was to live. Furthermore, he was told if he disobeyed, he would die. Man knows when he sins against a holy God. His eyes opened, and his conscience revealed that sin cost much more than he could bear. Adam and Eve were created God-centered, but sin made them self-centered. Their moral nature changed to man serving himself rather than obeying God.[40]

Isaiah 43:7 says God created man for His glory. Yet man and some of the angels sought their own glory. How can it be that something created godly could become sin-cursed so quickly? If you look in the Bible, you will find every person is born with a sin nature. The Jewish people murmured against God after they had been delivered from slavery. Moses tells us in Deuteronomy 9:16, "You have turned aside quickly from the way which the LORD had commanded you." When something good happens in your life, how long does it take before it is just a shadow that hardly existed?

When Adam and Eve were driven out of the Garden of Eden, they took with them something they did not have when they were formed. They took with them a sin nature that has been passed down to all generations. In Psalm 51:5, we read, "I was brought forth in iniquity, and in sin my

---

[40] "Man," *The Bible Pictorial Dictionary.*

mother conceived me." This physical body in which I dwell was shaped in sin from the time I was born. We all have that heritage. Jesus Christ is the only person who can remove that sin curse from us.

Before God destroyed the earth with a flood, He saw the wickedness of man was great in the earth. In Genesis 6:5, we read, "The Lord saw that the wickedness of man was great in the earth, and that every intent of the thoughts of his heart was only evil continually." Adam and Eve saw something they thought would make them wiser and better, but it did neither. In less than two thousand years from creation, God destroyed the world with a great flood. Eight people and all animal life, male and female, were saved from the flood. It was God's plan for there to be male and female of all life to replenish the earth. He punished the wickedness of man once. Do you not believe that He could do it again?

Throughout the Bible, man's character is revealed. The Bible tells us in Job 14:1, "Man who is born of woman is of a few days and full of trouble." In Judges 21:25, we read that in those days, every man did that which he thought was right in his own heart. Every person will justify his lifestyle to satisfy his own desires. The Bible can show each of us the meaning and purpose of life and minimize the troubles we will encounter in our lives. God has given man laws in which to live. If you do what you want in life, will all your problems go away? Has man's approach to life solved his problems? Satan and one-third of the angels were cast out of heaven because they wanted to live their way. The Bible tells us what is down every road of life. Furthermore, it tells us the kind of person we will become depending upon the direction we choose.

In Exodus 20:3–17, God gave Moses and the Jewish people the Ten Commandments to live by. Those commandments were to guide man in his walk throughout life. There are consequences for breaking society's law, and there will be consequences for breaking God's law. However, man has no fear of God or His laws. Every law God gave to man was for his good and to guide him throughout life. Laws are just words on paper if they are not heeded.

In Proverbs 1:5, the Bible says a wise man will hear and increase learning by seeking wise counsel. In verse 24, we read that God has called us to knowledge, but man has refused. God will not make us choose His way, but we do not get to choose the consequences of bad decisions. The Bible tells us in Proverbs 14:12, "There is a way that seems right to man, but its end is the way of death." Adam chose the road of disobedience. His life changed from immortality to the grave, from Paradise to the sweat of man's brow, from total peace with God to separation from Him, and from total joy to a heavy burden of sin. Even though man has chosen to be different from what God intended, His hand is always stretched out to man.

When we look at people, we only see the outer shell, and usually, that is all we allow others to see. The Bible tells us in 1 Samuel 16:7 that God sees our hearts. Then, who is man? It is time to take off the paint and clothes we cover ourselves with and peel back enough layers of the skin to reveal the heart. Then we can see who man really is. The Bible describes man perfectly; do you want to know? Down in that deepest, darkest part of your heart and soul is the person you really are. Do you dare look in the Bible to see who you are? The Bible will give you a guided tour.

As I read the Bible, I see two distinct problems or natures of every person: he has a heart problem and a flesh problem. You could say that everything about his nature comes from his heart; however, to explain the character of man in more detail, I have separated these two natures. I will focus on his heart first, then describe how he lives.

THE HEART OF MAN: HIS REBELLION

In the beginning, Adam and Eve rebelled against God. They were formed perfect but became corrupt and returned to the dust from which they came. We do not know how many years Adam and Eve walked with God in the Garden of Eden until they disobeyed Him. In Genesis 5:5, we read that Adam lived 930 years and then died. You may ask how someone could live that long. Adam and Eve were created before there was any sin. The world in which they lived was perfect as well. They lived in Paradise until sin entered their hearts. Where does sin and rebellion have its roots in man? We learn as children to rebel, and we seek ways to have our needs met. We learn to become self-centered at a very early stage in our lives. We all become selfish over time, seeking some form of attention. We learn early in life that we do not like to follow directions or be told what to do. The Bible tells us in Romans 13:1, "Let every soul be subject to governing authorities." Rebellion is defined as opposition to authority.[41] It is an act of defiance. People are not made to disobey; they choose not to follow rules and laws.

Rebellion began in the Bible before man was created. Ezekiel 28:15 tells us Satan was created. He did not exist in eternity with God. He exalted himself as being god and was cast out of heaven. The serpent (Satan) was in the Garden of Eden when Adam and Eve were placed there. He lied to them, and they were deceived. John 8:44 tells us the devil is a murderer and liar, and there is no truth in him. God and Satan were in the Garden of Eden and presented to Adam and Eve life and death. Nothing has changed since creation; each person will choose either God and life or disobedience and death. Each person is led to believe in something; we are not driven. Deception is all around us, and rebellion is common to every person. God gave each one of us a free will to obey or rebel.

Rebellion comes from man's heart. In Exodus 32:9, we read that the Lord told Moses the people were "stiff-necked." The people were stubborn. If you are around people long, you will see they can change behaviors quickly. 1 Samuel 15:22–23 says, "Has the Lord as great delight in burnt offerings and sacrifices, as in obeying the voice of the LORD? Behold, to obey is better than sacrifice, and to heed than the fat of rams. For rebellion is as the sin of witchcraft, and stubbornness is as iniquity and idolatry." Our offerings to God are meaningless if we do not obey His laws. In Isaiah 1:2, we read that God brought out a nation from Egypt and nourished them, but they rebelled against Him. Solomon tells us in Proverbs 1:24,

---

[41] "Rebellion," *The American Heritage Dictionary of the English Language.*

"I have called and you refused, I have stretched out my hand and no one regarded."

Man willfully chooses from his heart to disobey God. The Bible says in Psalm 52:3 that man loves evil more than good, and he would rather lie than speak the truth. James 1:8 says a double-minded man is unstable in all his ways. Man wants to cling to God and the devil at the same time. Jeremiah 5:3 says God chastises His people, but it does not affect them. They did not grieve nor repent of their sins. They were punished but refused to receive correction. Instead of having a heart receptive to God, their hearts became hardened. In Jeremiah 17:23, the Bible tells us they did not want to hear the voice of God or receive His instructions. We live in a time in which a lot of people do not like to be told what to do.

The Pharisees came to Jesus to ask Him why divorce was allowed. Jesus told them in Mark 10:2–6 that it was because of the "hardness of their hearts." God did not create divorce; man did. Stephen tells the people in Acts 7:51 that every person resists the Holy Spirit because He convicts us of our evil ways. We do not want to be told or shown we have sin in our lives. From man's heart, he reveals who he is. Romans 8:13 tells us if we fulfill the desires of the flesh, we will die. Furthermore, Psalm 66:18 says if we have sin in our hearts, the Lord will not hear us when we pray. Do you ever think about why your prayers are not answered?

I believe Satan has so deceived the people of this world that they do not know what to believe. Deception is getting stronger and stronger every day we live. In 2 Corinthians 4:4, Paul tells us Satan has blinded the minds of the people who do not believe. The light of Jesus Christ is shining, but the people refuse to open their eyes and see. Satan opposes everything that is true and righteous.

Every person wants to live his life in a way that pleases himself. The Bible says in Titus 1:16 that man professes to know God, but he denies Him in how he lives. Many people will tell you they believe in God but not Jesus Christ. The Bible tells us in 1 John 2:23 that whoever denies the Son (Jesus Christ) does not have the Father (God). If you claim to know God and not know Jesus Christ, you do not know the Bible. The Bible tells us God is Spirit, and Jesus Christ is God in human flesh. If you do not open your eyes and see the light of Jesus Christ, you will continue to follow a path of eternal damnation. Every one of us is led to believe in something; we choose what we want to believe.

Solomon tells us in Proverbs 1:25 that the reason people do not know the way and the truth is because they have refused His counsel and chastisement. In Proverbs 15:32, we read that he who refuses instruction despises his own soul. Isaiah 30:9 says rebellious people will not hear the law of the Lord. Every law God gives to us is for our good, but we cannot see God's goodness. The Bible says in Hosea 4:6 that God's people are destroyed for lack of knowledge because they have rejected truth. When we reject truth and knowledge, we are drawn to lies and evil. Man alone does not have the knowledge, heart, or will to combat the tricks Satan uses on every person. None of us can stand against Satan without God's help.

Jesus asks in John 7:19, "Did not Moses give you the law, yet none of you keeps the law?" 1 Peter 2:13 tells us to submit ourselves to the ordinances of man for the Lord's sake. Whether they are God-given or man-given, laws are for our guidance and good. God instructs us to obey the laws of our country. Do you obey all the laws? The Bible tells us in James 2:10 that whoever shall keep the law and yet offends in one area is guilty of breaking all laws. Have you ever lied to anyone? Do you covet things? Have you ever stolen anything, even if it was of little value? People want to categorize sin as little and big. Every sin we commit separates us from God. Rebellion is in the heart of everyone who willfully disobeys the law.

You may feel you did not intend to break the law. You just drifted along with the wrong crowd. The Bible tells us in Psalm 106:35 that the people mingled among the heathen and learned their ways. You may believe you can be with anyone and not be affected by their ways. You become like the people you associate with; they do not change—you do. The Bible gives us explicit warnings about the kinds of people we are to be around. We choose who we associate with; we are not made to be with anyone.

Are you prone to rebel against all laws and authority? Is there a standard from which you respond to rules and laws? Is popular opinion or being politically correct the answer? The Bible tells us in Romans 1:25 that the people exchanged the truth of God for a lie, and they worshipped and served the creature rather than the Creator. In verse 28, we read that man does not want to retain God in his mind. Therefore, He has given them over to a corrupt mind to do those things of their lusts. Paul tells us in 2 Timothy 4:3 that the time will come when man will not hear the truth but will seek his own desires. In 2 Peter 2:15, we find that man has forsaken the right way and has gone the way of idolatry and the devil.

From the beginning, man has stumbled over the truth and the Bible. The Bible says in Amos 8:11 that the day is coming when there will be a famine in the land, not of food or water, but of hearing God's Word and the truth. I saw an article in my local newspaper a few weeks ago that said almost one-half of the people do not know what is true, regardless of the news source. Has the famine started?

Man has chosen to rebel against God, not for a lack of knowledge. He knows who God is, but he willingly disobeys Him. The Bible tells us we cannot serve two masters (Matthew 6:24). Do you trust what your heart tells you to do? Jeremiah 17:9 says, "The heart is deceitful above all things and beyond cure. Who can know it?" Do you have a heart problem? Are you rebelling against truth and the law? Jesus Christ is the only person who can change your heart.

THE HEART OF MAN: HIS PRIDE

Why do you think pride is such a big problem with God? Pride is defined as a sense of your own self, identity, and value.[42] You can have pride in your family, work, and any achievement. There is nothing wrong with having some forms of pride. The problem with pride, however, is when you exalt yourself as being better than others and God. The Bible tells us in Proverbs

---

[42] "Pride," *The American Heritage Dictionary of the English Language.*

6:16–19, "These six things the Lord hates, yes, seven are an abomination to Him." The very first thing listed is a proud look. If pride is something meaningful to man, why does God hate it?

I do not believe God is angry with people for some forms of pride. I believe the hate God has against pride goes back to before man ever existed. Satan is a created fallen angel. The Bible tells us Satan was the most beautiful angel created. Because of his beauty, he exalted himself and wanted to be above God. Ezekiel 28:17 says he corrupted himself because of his beauty and brightness. He was cast down to earth to deceive kings and nations. God's plan to redeem man is through Jesus Christ and not through anything created.

When you read the Bible, you will find man's pride is usually described as sinful. He wants the praise of other men; he wants to be exalted above other people. Jesus tells us in Matthew 18:3–4 that unless you become as a little child, you cannot see the kingdom of heaven. Every person who has come to Christ humbled himself at one time. Christ does not want you to humble yourself as a slave to a master; He wants your love. Jesus told Nicodemus if he wanted to see the kingdom of heaven, he must be born again. Is pride keeping you from coming to Christ?

We know the source of man's pride; what is the source of your pride? What do you put ahead of God, and does it give you perfect peace and joy in your soul and sustain you through the trials of everyday life?

In Psalm 49:6, we read that man cannot trust in his wealth. The Bible says in Psalm 73:6 that pride is like a chain that covers us. In Proverbs 7:26, we see pride will tell us that we can play around with sin and not be slain. Pride will tell us everything is okay in our own eyes. In Proverbs 16:18, we read that pride goes before destruction. Because of man's pride, he will sin and say, "I have done no wickedness" (Proverbs 30:20). Furthermore, Isaiah 3:9 says man will sin and will no longer try to hide it. When people can no longer see their sins, they will walk in their own self-righteousness. Man has a problem with his thinking, however; he thinks he can continually sin and find peace in his life. Jeremiah 8:15 tells us the opposite: We looked for peace, but there was trouble!

As man continues in his path of sinful living, Zephaniah 3:5 tells us the unjust know no shame. In Romans 10:3, we read that people do not want the righteousness of God. They want to establish their own way to live. The Bible says in Jeremiah 17:5, "Cursed is the man who trusts in man and makes flesh his strength, whose heart departs from the LORD." Where do you turn for help—is your strength in man?

What is the path man takes in which he becomes prideful? In Ezekiel 16:49, we read that when man is full of bread and has an abundance of idleness, he becomes full of pride. Hosea 13:6 says the people were filled, and their hearts were exalted. When we are full, we feel we do not need God. Obadiah 3 says, "The pride of your heart has deceived you . . . whose habitation is high; you say in your heart, 'Who will bring me down to the ground?'" We read in Jeremiah 49:16 that pride will take us to the highest hill, but God will bring us down. Furthermore, in 1 Timothy 6:4, we find that the prideful person knows nothing but evil and strife. Titus 3:3–4 says we were once foolish, disobedient, deceived, lustful, looking for pleasure in life, living in sin, envious, and full of hate for other people before we became Christians. Every person has the same beginning, but some people come to the light of Jesus Christ when they see it. Others will walk away from that light.

Man thinks no one sees his sins. The Bible tells us in Jeremiah 16:17 that God's eyes are on all of the ways of men; they are not hidden from His face, nor is their iniquity hidden from His eyes. Can we not see in our hearts the God who created us knows everything about us? There are no dark places to hide our sins. In Hosea 7:2, we read that God not only knows our hearts but He also remembers all of man's wickedness.

Matthew 6:21 says, "For where your treasure is, there your heart will be also." Are the things in our lives our treasure? Do they bring happiness and joy to our hearts and souls? Matthew 23:12 reads, "Whoever exalts himself will be humbled, and he who humbles himself will be exalted." Solomon says in Proverbs 15:33 that before honor, there is humility. The world says, "Look at me; see what I have done." We have done very little; Jesus Christ gave His life for you and me.

Do you desire the praise of man more than anything? Satan will tell you to exalt yourself and boast about who you are. The Bible says to humble yourself before God, and He will exalt you.

Humility is defined as being meek, modest, having self-control, and being submissive.[43] Jesus uses the word servant as someone who is humble. When Jesus was born, it was in a stable, not a mansion. The Bible tells us in Philippians 2:8 that Jesus fashioned Himself as a man and humbled Himself and became obedient to death on the cross. He did not have to start His life in a barn, nor did He have to die on the cross. Whenever you humble yourself, you are placing others before yourself. Jesus showed all of us how to put others before ourselves.

The Bible tells us in Psalm 10:17 that the Lord hears the desires of the humble. In James 4:10, we read, "Humble yourselves in the sight of the Lord, and He will lift you up." Solomon tells us in Proverbs 22:4, "By humility and the fear of the LORD are riches and honor and life." Being humble goes against everything the world teaches us to do. The Bible, however, tells us the greatest treasures in life will come to us if we are humble. The world will tell us to take care of number one—ourselves. Jesus and the Bible tell us to prefer others before ourselves. Who is number one in your life?

Most people believe there is nothing free in life. There are many people who believe you have to earn your way to heaven. By not knowing the Bible, man's pride can lead him to believe things that are not true. You cannot buy your way to heaven. Furthermore, many people believe if your goodness is better than your badness, you will go to heaven. You will not find that said anywhere in the Bible. Your church, family, recognition, and praise by man will not get you there. Your name and status in society do not make any difference to God. Is it man's pride that keeps him from seeking the truth, or is he so deceived by Satan he does not want to know? The Bible tells us in Ephesians 2:8–9, "For by grace you are saved through faith, and that not of yourselves; it is the gift of God, not of works, lest

---

[43] "Humility," *The American Heritage Dictionary of the English Language.*

anyone should boast." People want to brag about their accomplishments and compare themselves to others to validate in their hearts that they are better people. Because of man's pride, he will rationalize his goodness to others. Only in the Bible will we find the playing surface to be totally level. We are either Jew or Gentile, male or female; there are no other categories.

Because of man's pride, he has a lack of knowledge and does not know salvation is free. We can boast to others and say, "Look what I have done," but honor and real life come through humbling ourselves before God and others.

THE HEART OF MAN: HIS CONSCIENCE

When God breathed the breath of life into man, he became a moral being. The Bible tells us God created mankind with a soul (Genesis 2:6) and a conscience (Romans 2:15). A conscience is defined as recognizing the distinction between right and wrong in regard to one's conduct.[44] The *Pictorial Bible Dictionary* says all men are responsible for their actions before God because we all have a revelation of God's moral law. From the beginning, man has known right from wrong. When Adam and Eve disobeyed God, their conscience revealed to them they were naked. If you claim to be a Christian and sin against God, your conscience will tell you of your sin. Sin cannot coexist together with the Holy Spirit in the same place in your soul. The Bible tells us in 1 Timothy 4:2 that Christians know when they sin unless their conscience has been seared. Does your conscience ever bother you?

In Proverbs 4:23, we read, "Keep your heart with all diligence, for out of it spring the issues of life." The Bible tells us in 1 Corinthians 8:7–12 that our conscience should guide us in how we live before other people. In Acts 9:18, Saul found going against Jesus Christ was a sin load his conscience could not bear. Jesus asked the scribes and Pharisees in John 8:3–7, "He who is without sin among you, let him throw a stone at her first."

[44] "Conscience," *The American Heritage Dictionary of the English Language.*

They all walked away because their conscience revealed sin within their own hearts. We cannot stand in the presence of Christ and judge another person. If we live in sin, Titus 1:15 tells us our minds and conscience are defiled.

Do you believe Christians should not sin? The Bible says in Romans 7:23 that there is a war in man's mind. The battle is between the Spirit of God and the sin nature of our flesh. Galatians 5:17 says the flesh lusts against the Spirit and the Spirit against the flesh because they are contrary to each other. As long as Christians live, the Holy Spirit will dwell in a sin-cursed physical body.

Every person has a moral compass to guide them. You may want to blame others for the circumstances in your life; however, each person chooses the direction he will take in his life. You were not created with a blank slate for a mind. You were created in the image and likeness of a holy and righteous God. You know right from wrong, and the path you are taking in life did not come about by accident; choices were made.

THE HEART OF MAN: PEACE AND DESPAIR

Is peace the absence of war? People and nations want peace, but how do we find and keep it? Adversity and circumstances of life do not determine our peace. Our relationship with Jesus Christ is the key to the peace we can have in our hearts. The Bible says in Ecclesiastes 4:1 that oppressors have power, but they have no comfort. The people who are oppressed have tears, but they have no comforter. In Jeremiah 6:14, we read that the people cry for peace "when there is no peace." Lamentations 5:5 says that man labors, but he has no rest. Are you looking for comfort and rest from the routine of daily life? Isaiah 57:21 tells us there is no peace for the wicked. When adversity happens in life, do you seek God? Or is God the last place you look for comfort?

Real peace can only come from God. Man is to reflect God to everyone he encounters. But man cannot get along with people at home, at work, or as nations. Nations are crumbling because the home is broken. The Bible says in Isaiah 26:3 that God will keep you in perfect peace if your mind is stayed upon Him. Are you searching for peace and rest in life, or are you only finding despair?

The Bible tells us in Psalm 88:1–3 that man cries day and night for God because his soul is full of trouble. Why does man live in so much despair and sorrow? Despair is defined as losing all hope and having a sense of defeat.[45] Suicide was the twelfth leading cause of death in the United States in 2020.[46] Is killing yourself the only option left when you lose hope? The word suicide is not stated in the Bible; however, there are times in which someone took their own life. Solomon tells us in Ecclesiastes 2:17 that he hated life because everything he did was distressing and empty. He says in Ecclesiastes 2:23, "All his days are sorrowful, and his work burdensome; even in the night his heart takes no rest." Are all your tomorrows filled with questions?

The Bible tells us in Daniel 9:11 that if we transgress God's law, we will have a curse on our lives. People think they can break God's laws and then run to Him anytime they want. Ezekiel 39:24 says, "According to their uncleanness and according to their transgressions I have dealt with them, and hidden My face from them." Are you in despair because you feel God has hidden His face from you? Jeremiah tells us in Lamentations 1:22 that mankind has many sins, and his heart becomes faint when he tries to carry his burdens and sins alone.

The Bible says in Psalm 61:2, "When my heart is overwhelmed; lead me to the rock that is higher than I." When the psalmist is overwhelmed, he cries out to God. Are you seeking real help or just a temporary solution to your problems? Jesus tells us in Matthew 15:8, "These people draw near to Me with their mouth . . . but their heart is far from Me." God knows

---

[45] "Despair," *The American Heritage Dictionary of the English Language.*

[46] Sally C. Curtin, M.A., et al, "Deaths Leading Causes for 2020," *National Vital Statistic Reports* 72, no. 13 (December 5, 2023): 13.

the intent of your heart. God wants to be your refuge, and His arms are always outstretched to you.

Before Jesus was crucified, He tells us in John 14:1,3, "Let not your heart be troubled; you believe in God, believe also in Me. And if I go and prepare a place for you, I will come again and receive you to Myself." Sin is a burden for the heart to bear. If we choose to carry it alone, sorrow and despair will walk along with us.

Are you carrying a heavy burden? Are you losing hope? You don't have to carry that sin load anymore. Jesus Christ can totally change your heart and set you free.

I have tried to tell you from the Bible about the heart of mankind. All sin has its roots in the heart. What about the flesh that bears that sin's nature? The Bible tells us in Ephesians 2:3 that everyone in the past walked in the lusts of their flesh and were, by nature, the children of wrath. In Galatians 4:14, we read that temptation comes from our flesh. Paul tells us in Galatians 5:19–21 that the works of the flesh are these: adultery, fornication, uncleanness, lasciviousness, idolatry, witchcraft, hatred, variance, emulations, wrath, strife, sedition, heresy, envy, murder, drunkenness and reveling. Each person sins in many ways, yet he will tell you he is a good person.

THE FLESH OF MAN: HIS GOODNESS

Solomon tells us in Ecclesiastes 7:20, "There is not a just man on earth who does good and does not sin." So why does man think he is a good person when the Bible says otherwise? Is that which was created more knowledgeable than the Creator? Solomon tells us in Proverbs 16:2, "All the ways of man are pure in his own eyes." He tells us in Proverbs 30:12 that there is a generation of people who are pure in their own hearts, but they have not washed themselves from their filthiness. As time goes on, does man think he becomes better than his ancestors? Jeremiah 2:35 says that man feels he is innocent and does not sin. The Bible tells us in Isaiah 5:20–21,

"Woe to those who call evil good, and good evil . . . Woe to those who are wise in their own eyes." How, then, does man justify he is a good person?

We read in Ezekiel 16:51 that man will try to justify his behavior in any sinful thing he tries to do. Luke 7:36–39 says that the educated and those in a high position feel they are better than others of lesser knowledge or position. Jesus tells us in Luke 18:9 that the Pharisees trusted "in themselves that they were righteous, and despised others." Solomon says in Proverbs 20:6, "Most men will proclaim each his own goodness." The Bible tells us every person is born in sin, so where did the self-righteousness come from? When does a man become a good person? Because man thinks he is a good person, he believes there are many ways to get to heaven. John 14:6 tells us, however, that Jesus is the *only* way to heaven.

In Romans 1:22, we read that men claim to be wise, but instead, they become fools. When God gave man a soul, he knew then what was right and wrong. Is that when man began to think that everything he did was right and there was no wrong? Amos 6:1 warns that there is woe to a man who is at ease with the sinful life he is living and trusts in himself. The problem every person has in claiming his goodness is he compares himself to others. We want to vindicate ourselves as being better than most people. All men, however, are unclean in the presence of a holy God (Isaiah 6:5). God has set the standard for righteousness, not man. The Bible tells us in Isaiah 64:6 what we are compared to His holiness—all our righteousness is as filthy rags. Those filthy rags were the rags taken from someone who has leprous skin that drained throughout the day. I don't think any person knows what true holiness and purity are, so we look at other people and try to justify our goodness. Jesus tells us in Luke 13:26–27 that there are people who think they are doing great things for God. He tells them, "I do not know you." You may be able to fool the people you are around, and they may think you are a good person. God fashioned your heart, however, and He knows who you are. Are you still looking in the mirror?

THE FLESH OF MAN: KNOWLEDGE, TRUTH, AND FOOLISHNESS

From the time he's a baby until he dies, man is exposed to information that will affect the decisions he makes throughout life. Solomon tells us in Proverbs 1:7, "The fear of the Lord is the beginning of knowledge." If you remove God from education, where does man begin to learn? Knowledge is to know and to be aware of everything around us. Do schools expose our children to all knowledge or just what they want us to know? Fearing God means having a deep respect for God and His laws. Schools do not teach anything about creation, but they will teach evolution, which cannot be proven. If we are to know, we should be given the chance to discern information and make our own decisions. The question we need to ask ourselves is this: Do they want us to know?

What can we learn from the Bible about knowledge? Do you want to know? The wisest person in the Bible, Solomon, tells us in Proverbs 1:22 that "fools hate knowledge." Do you want to attain knowledge and know, or would you rather be a fool?

Solomon tells us in Ecclesiastes 1:13, "I set my heart to seek and search out by wisdom concerning all that is done under heaven." Does not man try to do the same in seeking answers from all things? He wants to know, but he does not want to know about God and creation. In Job 11:7, we read, "Can you search out the deep things of God?" Is that the reason man does not search all things—he does not want God? We do not have to search to know good and evil. Even though we know sin, Jeremiah 10:23 says the way of man is not in himself to direct his own steps. Jesus tells us in Mark 8:12 that man seeks signs to know what to do." He will turn to any source he can find seeking advice but never turn to his Creator. In 1 Corinthians 1:20–21, we read that the world's wisdom does not know God. "Has not God made foolish the wisdom of this world?" Jeremiah 8:9 tells us there is no wisdom apart from what God gives. The Bible tells us in Psalm 119:105, "Your word is a lamp to my feet and a light to my path." Are you getting wise counsel from the world's wisdom, or are you seeking signs to guide you in life?

The opportunity to attain knowledge is everywhere we are. All we have to do is open our eyes and ears, and we are exposed to it; however, can we discern the knowledge we receive to know if it is true? Solomon tells us in Proverbs 23:9, "Do not speak in the hearing of a fool, for he will despise the wisdom of your words." He tells us in Proverbs 12:15, "The way of a fool is right in his own eyes." Man attempts to know all things except what is true. We have come to a time in the United States when almost half the people no longer know what is true. There is no truth in any person. God and the Bible are the only absolute standards for truth.

The Bible tells us in Isaiah 59:14, "Truth is fallen in the street." In Jeremiah 23:36, we read that man has perverted the Word of God so that he does not believe it. Furthermore, Jeremiah 7:28 says truth has perished. The Bible tells us very plainly that lying is a sin; however, we know people want to categorize sin as big and little. Is there not a standard for truth anymore in the world we live in? We read in 2 Peter 2:2 that man will follow his own evil way because the way of truth will be blasphemed. Do we not want truth in our lives, or would we rather believe a lie? To be knowledgeable, we should be able to discern what is true. In John 1:1, the Bible says, "In the beginning was the Word, and the Word was with God, and the Word was God." There is a standard for truth whether man believes it or not. The Bible is true because it is God. Furthermore, the Bible is complete and has everything in it to guide us through life. Where is our greatest source of knowledge; is it from man? If there is no truth in man, where will you turn? Fools will not seek truth; are you a fool?

Today, the internet is a source for attaining knowledge. The Bible says in 2 Timothy 3:7 that man is always learning, but he is "never able to come to the knowledge of truth." Is the Bible too hard to understand? Psalm 119:130 tells us the Bible gives light and understanding to the simple. Is it so simple people stumble over it, or does it reveal man's sinful heart? The world's wisdom does not want to know God. Paul tells us in 2 Timothy 4:3 that the time will come when man will not want to know truth; he would rather follow his own desires. Jeremiah 4:22 tells us man is wise to do evil, but he does not want the knowledge to do good. In Isaiah 9:2, the Bible says that every person walked in the darkness at one time, but they have seen a great light. That great light is revealed to every person. God manifests Himself to everyone's soul and spirit. Everyone sees that light in his soul, and he will either walk toward it or walk away. All of us are plugged into a far greater source of knowledge and truth than the internet. Truth and light help us to see and guide us in every area of life. But the light exposes everything we don't want to see. Is that why man likes to stay in the dark?

Man will seek to know the why of all things in life; however, he does not want to know God. He wants some light and knowledge, but only part of the truth. He knows he cannot stand in the presence of pure truth and light. Therefore, he does not want to know Jesus Christ personally. Furthermore, man cannot come to Christ through the knowledge of the world. The Bible tells us in 1 Corinthians 2:5 that we come to Christ though faith, not in the wisdom of man.

We have unlimited sources of knowledge that are accessible to each of us. Paul tells us in 2 Thessalonians 2:3 that the day is coming when man will be easily deceived. Where do we go to find truth if not all knowledge is true? There is a standard for truth, but we will not find it in man. Solomon tells us the fear of the Lord is the beginning of knowledge. The beginning did not start when man was created from the dust of the earth. The beginning was when God said, "I Am."

THE FLESH OF MAN: TEMPTATION AND DECEPTION

What comes to your mind when you think of temptation? James 1:13 reads that God does not tempt anyone with evil. If you have evil thoughts with temptation, it is coming from your heart. When God tempted Abraham in

Genesis 22:1, He was testing his faith. Paul tells us in 1 Corinthians 10:13, "No temptation has overtaken you except such as is common to man; but God is faithful, who will not allow you to be tempted beyond what you are able, but with the temptation, will also make the way of escape, that you may be able to bear it." God may test your faith, but He will not use sin to find out how much you love Him.

Solomon tells us in Proverbs 12:26 that wicked men will lead us to evil and sin. Jesus tells us in Matthew 26:41, "Watch and pray, lest you enter into temptation. The Spirit indeed is willing, but the flesh is weak." The Bible tells us in Romans 8:6 that to be carnally or fleshly minded is death. Paul tells us in 1 Thessalonians 5:22 that we are to "abstain from every form of evil." Something as little as its appearance can lead us down the road to sin.

All advertising is directed toward your senses. Typically, that which you see is more appealing and seductive; however, anything that stimulates your mind to think about it will produce its desired effect. Sin's appearance connects with man's desires, often producing behaviors that were not planned. Paul says in 2 Timothy 3:5–6 that sin's appeal may have a form of godliness, but it denies the power of God. It creeps into your life and leads you away to your own desires. Man is tempted when he is enticed by the desires of his heart. The appeal of sin draws man away from his intended purpose.

The Bible says in 1 John 2:16, "For all that is in the world—the lust of the flesh, the lust of the eyes, and the pride of life—is not of the Father but is of the world." Solomon tells us in Proverbs 7:19–27 that a good man went on a journey and was tempted by an adulterous woman. She used flattering words to entice him and led him away as an ox to the slaughter. Many strong men have been slain by her. Man thinks he can play with temptation and not get hurt. Jesus tells us in Matthew 5:28, "Whoever looks at a woman to lust for her has already committed adultery with her in his heart." Sin's appeal will draw us to it often before we realize what happened. The Bible says in Ezekiel 20:7 that we are to cast away the abominations of our eyes and not defile ourselves with idols. We under-estimate how some temptations appeal to our hearts. If we do not walk away from sin immediately, we can be drawn to it so easily. Are you easily drawn to sin?

I was looking recently at my channel guide of television shows and noticed there is a show called *American Greed*. It tells about people who will go to any measure to attain what they want. God gave Moses and the Jewish people Ten Commandments in which to live. Exodus 20:17 tells us to not covet. Solomon says in Proverbs 1:19 that if someone is greedy to gain, it will take away the life of its owners. In Ezekiel 22:13, we read that God knows about the dishonest gain taken by the shedding of blood. How many people are incarcerated in jails today because they coveted something they did not have and stole it? The Bible warns us in Habakkuk 2:6, "Woe to him who increases what is not his." Paul says in Ephesians 2:3 that we are to not seek after the desires and lusts of the flesh. How often do we lust for things we cannot get? The tenth commandment God gave to us instructed man to not covet.

When you hear the word "world," what comes to your mind? Jesus tells us in John 17:14 that believers are not of this world. Most of the time, when the Bible is talking about the world, it is talking about a philosophy of life that does not include God. It is usually talking about the devil's influence on how people live. How does the world influence you in the decisions you make in life?

The Bible tells the Jewish people in Deuteronomy 12:30 to not be snared by following after the ways of the people who live there when they enter into the Promised Land. God warned His people to avoid and not mix with the inhabitants of the land. God knew if they associated with the people of the land, they would become like them. They would lead the Jewish people to idolatry. When we become obsessed with what the world presents to us, we take our eyes off Christ. The Bible says in John 1:10 that Christ "was in the world, and the world was made through Him, and the world did not know Him." This world's philosophy does not want

Jesus Christ. Jesus tells us in John 7:7 that the world hates Him because He testifies of the world's evil. Man's world is not a good place to live. Jesus tells us in John 14:17 that the world will not receive truth because it does not know Him. They know about God, but they do not know Jesus Christ.

There are far too many people in this world who think they can live in sin and still be in good standing with God. In James 4:4, the Bible says if we are friends with the world, we are an enemy of God. John tells us in 1 John 5:19 that the whole world is under the influence of the wicked one. Throughout the Bible, we read God is holy and righteous. If we think we can live a worldly life and live for God at the same time, this world has us deceived.

Jesus tells us in John 14:30, "The ruler of this world is coming, and he has nothing in Me." The Bible says in John 1:5, Light shines in the darkness, and the darkness does not want the light. Man had rather stay in the dark. This world is a dark place; where are you looking for directions? The influence of Satan (the devil) is everywhere in the world. You may think there is no such thing as the devil. The Bible tells us there is a devil, and he is the reason the world is filled with sin and evil. If mankind is evolving, why is this world filled with so much evil?

Satan has far more influence on unbelievers than they realize. The Bible says in Genesis 3:1 that he was more cunning than any beast God had made. We read in Mark 13:22, "False Christs and false prophets who will come forth and show signs and wonders to deceive you from knowing the truth." He claimed to have authority, but only God has total authority. By the death and resurrection of Jesus Christ, Satan knows he only has a short time to deceive the people.

Man is a created being, just as Satan is. Satan knows how to deceive and lie to man. Paul tells us in 2 Thessalonians 2:9–10 that the power of Satan is present in the world with signs and lying wonders. He uses deception to seduce people because they have not received the truth that could save them. The Bible reveals to us in 2 Corinthians 4:4 that Satan has blinded the minds of the people. They do not believe it could be as simple as going toward a light. In 1 John 3:8 we read, whosoever continually sins is of the devil. Do you continually live in sin?

THE FLESH OF MAN: SEX AND LUSTS

Paul tells us in Ephesians 4:27 that we are not to let the devil have a place in our hearts. Every day of life, we will face temptation and the appeal of sin. Movies, television, and most advertising have sexual or sensual connotations. Can we not see the progression of how sex is portrayed in everything we are around? I can remember back in the 1950s, television shows portrayed married couples sleeping in separate beds. Now, many people sleep together the first time they meet. We may think the sins today are different than they used to be, but Solomon tells us in Ecclesiastes 1:9 that there is nothing new under heaven. Media sources try to present sin differently. Deception is the key. Sin is noted in just the third chapter of the Bible. The heart of man has never changed. Sex was not a sin when God created Adam and Eve; however, sin took away the innocence from the world in which they lived. God created the sexual relationship between husband and wife as good, but man changed it into his own lusts and desires.

The Bible says in James 3:15 that sensual, demonic desires do not come from God. In Exodus 20:14, we read the seventh commandment God gave to Moses and the Jewish people: "You shall not commit adultery." God gave the people other laws regarding their sexual behavior in Leviticus 18:6–22. The sexual relationship was created clean between a man and a woman. In 2 Peter 2:10, we read that we are not to walk in the unclean lusts of the flesh. Paul tells us in 2 Timothy 3:3 that many people will be without self-control. Romans 1:27 says men have left the natural use of the woman and burn in lust for another man. Men with men and women with women, committing that which is shameful. It is commonplace in this country for men to marry men and women to marry women. The Bible says that kind of relationship is "unnatural." We read in Romans 6:16 that to whom we yield ourselves slaves to obey, that we obey, whether to sin and sexual lusts or to righteousness. Man is a sexual being, but God has warned us about how we are to live. The Bible tells us in James 4:1–2 that we will have problems in life when we lust and war within our own souls. We lust and have not; we kill and desire to have and cannot attain. How far will man go in his desires?

Do your lusts have control over your life?

Every person has a set point of knowing right and wrong. When you lust to have something, how long does it make you happy? The Bible says in Romans 1:24 that God gave man up to uncleanness in the lusts of his heart to dishonor his own body. Paul tells us in 1 Corinthians 6:18 that we are to flee sexual immorality because every sin man does is without the body, but he that commits fornication sins against his own body. Sex outside the marriage relationship damages us physically, emotionally, and spiritually. Man does not realize how much he destroys himself by the way he lives.

Solomon tells us in Proverbs 4:19 that the way of the wicked is in darkness. In Job 24:15–16, we read, "The eye of the adulterer waits for twilight, saying, 'No eye will see me.'" Everyone who does evil hates the light. He does not come into the light because he would be exposed. Furthermore, he will try to cover himself in the day. Man imagines all kinds of evil thoughts and evil deeds when it is dark. He thinks no one can see because of the darkness. In Psalm 139:15, we read that we were not hidden from God when we were conceived in secret. Man thinks if no one sees him, he did not do anything wrong. You can fool man: You can lie, cheat, and get away, but God knows everything you do. When you stand before God at the judgment, there will be nowhere to hide. You will be alone before God, and He will have the evidence.

THE FLESH OF MAN: MAN'S ATTEMPT TO ESCAPE REALITY

Have we come to a point in this world where deception and lies are commonplace? Is it easier for man to be fake? In Genesis 3:1, we read that the serpent (the devil) was more subtle than anything created. The dictionary defines subtle as a person who sometimes has problems discerning which way to turn. The Bible tells us exactly which way to go and how we are to live, but man wants to live his life his way.

The Bible says in Jeremiah 9:6 that man lives in the middle of deceit: "Through deceit they refuse to know Me." Man deliberately refuses to believe. Paul tells us in Galatians 6:3 that because of man's pride, he often deceives himself. Until you know God, you will never fully know how Satan deceives man. The Bible says in 1 Timothy 4:1 that in the end times, man will depart from the truth and give heed to deceiving spirits and doctrines of demons. The time is coming, and it may be now, in which man will believe a lie before he will believe the truth. You will not find truth in the world's philosophy of life. If you are deceived, you are walking down a dark path.

We live in a time in which people want a remote control or a pill to change reality and make their problems go away. Many, many people want more than a remote control; they want something to somehow make life more enjoyable. Alcohol and drugs are easy substances to entice and deceive man's thinking. The Bible has a lot to say about wine and strong drink; drugs are not mentioned. The Bible, however, tells us in Ecclesiastes that there is nothing new under heaven. I am sure people in Bible times used some form of substances to alter the reality of their life situation. How foolish and deceived man can be if he thinks by ingesting something into his body, he will no longer have to face the reality of his life's problems. Do we think the problem will be any less tomorrow than it is today? I know, too, that there are many people who drink that like alcohol, and it is commonplace in social settings.

What can we find in the Bible about man using wine and strong drink? Wine is referenced in 232 verses throughout the Bible. Strong drink is written about twenty-one times. The first miracle of Jesus was changing water into wine in John 2:1–11. We may think if Jesus turned water into wine, He occasionally drank Himself. The Bible does not say anywhere Jesus drank wine. When Jesus met with His disciples at the last supper, He told them He would not drink the fruit of the vine again until He drinks it with them in His Father's kingdom (Matthew 26:29). Why did Jesus use the words fruit of the vine? Grape juice is a fruit of the vine, as is wine, yet wine was not stated. I know there are many people who go to church and drink alcohol. My intent is to not pass judgment on any person's lifestyle but to reveal to us what is said about it in the Bible.

Whether you believe me or not, alcohol and mind-altering drugs have deceived men into believing life is better when they can escape reality. When alcohol is advertised, it is presented as the "one" item needed to make a gathering of people happy. If you need a substance of some kind to make you happy, you are a very shallow person. You will never be happy with the person you were created to be. Furthermore, you probably could never be at peace in your heart with Christ alone. The Bible tells us that in Christ, we can have a peace that passes all understanding (Philippians 4:7). Job tells us if we are born of woman, life will have its problems. If you are a believer, everything that has any meaning in life is in Jesus Christ, not in anything you desire from this world.

Television, movies, and multimedia sources depict alcohol as a necessary item for having a good time. Statistics from the 2018 National Institute of Alcohol Abuse and Alcoholism reveal that 56 percent of the people drank some form of alcohol the previous month. Of that number, 26.5 percent of those eighteen and over binge drank. Of adolescents aged twelve to seventeen, 2.5 percent had a drinking problem. In 2014, 88,000 people died with alcohol-related deaths. It was the third leading cause of preventable deaths in the United States. In fact, 31 percent of all driving fatalities were alcohol-related.

In 2010, alcohol problems resulted in the loss of 249 billion dollars of lost revenue. I worked in an alcohol and drug rehabilitation program in the late 1980s, and those people could tell you the number of families and homes alcohol destroyed. Death, disabilities, families destroyed, lost revenue, violent crimes, rape, heartache, and misery; does man really know what truly brings peace to his heart and soul? We seek happiness and answers to life from any source we can find, deceived into thinking a thing or substance will make us happy. Things or substances will never fill the soul God put into each one of us. Many states have now legalized marijuana, and it will be legal everywhere soon. It will not be legal because of its benefits but because of the tax revenue it will generate.

Right and wrong, good and evil, are of no significance to the world's philosophy of life. Money and power are what is important. People elected to represent us talk about the drug problem we have, thinking they can do something about it. There are two big reasons that will never happen. The biggest reason is there is too much money in high places to stop it. And man will always seek some form of substance to alter reality and escape from his circumstances. Does that substance actually change the situation, or is man so deceived in his thinking he no longer knows the path his life is taking? What does the Bible say about alcohol use?

The Bible gives man many more warnings about its use than its benefits. Solomon tells us in Proverbs 20:1 that wine is a mocker and strong drink is a brawler, and whoever is led astray by it is not wise. The Bible says in Isaiah 5:11 that the man who drinks all day until the night will be inflamed by it. I have been around people who get happy when they drink. But I have also been around many more people who want to conquer the world. Habakkuk 2:5 warns us about using wine to break the law and take advantage of others. Solomon tells us in Proverbs 23:31–33, "Do not look on the wine when it is red in the cup, when it sparkles in the cup, when it swirls around smoothly; at the last it bites like a serpent, and stings like a viper. Your eyes will see strange things, and your heart will utter perverse things."

The Bible says in Habakkuk 2:15, "Woe to him who gives his drink to his neighbor, pressing him to your bottle, even to make him drunk, that you may look on his nakedness." Solomon tells us in Proverbs 31:5 that if we use strong drink, we forget the law and pervert judgment. In Isaiah 28:7 we read that the priests who use wine and strong drink have erred in their vision and stumble in judgment.

Alcohol and many drugs have the capability of affecting the brain when it enters the bloodstream. Not all substances we ingest or that penetrate the skin enter into the blood. What happens to man when he takes alcohol and drugs into his body? For every three times the Bible says something about wine and strong drink, it says something about being drunk or some form of drunkenness. There are eighty-five times in the Bible that word is written about. The dictionary defines drunk as an impairment of physical and mental faculties. When you take something into your body, it may not make you drunk; however, it does enter the bloodstream and affects your brain. Another word you may prefer to use instead of drunkenness is inhibition. Inhibition means there is some form of restraint in your behavioral processes. Your ability to fully use all your capabilities is restrained. Regardless of how little or how much enters your body, it does enter your brain.

The Bible tells us in 1 Peter 5:8 to be sober and vigilant because our adversary, the devil, walks about as a roaring lion seeking whoever he may devour. What does it mean to be sober? Sober is characterized by self-control, being rational and reasonable. If we are vigilant, we are on the alert and watchful, fully aware of everything going on around us. We may say to ourselves, "It is only one or two beers; it will not affect me." It will get into our blood regardless of the amount and possibly impair our thinking and judgment.

Some people will tell you alcohol is beneficial to their well-being. Paul tells us in 1 Timothy 5:23 to use a little wine for our stomachs' sake. Man can pick and choose verses in the Bible to justify the life he wants to live. I do know people will consume alcohol just to feel accepted. The Bible tells us in 1 Corinthians 15:33, "Do not be deceived: 'Evil company corrupts good habits.'" I don't care how strong you are or how strong your values are; if you continually associate with a bad crowd, you will become like them. You gain respect and become somebody when you do something different. When you give in to peer pressure, you are allowing others to dictate how you want to live. You forfeit your rights to other people. When you give in to their desires, they will use you for their benefit. They will take everything of value from you, including your self-respect. If you conform to the crowd, you are letting the world know their values are better than yours. I can remember, at the age of twenty-four, my first experience of being around people using marijuana. I did not participate with the crowd. Later, someone told me they respected my feelings for being different. Everyone needs to know that when God created each one of us, He made us different. Regardless of how much you may want to be like someone else, you are a unique creation of God. You are special in the eyes of God, just the way you are.

We all need to come to a place in life in which we build a foundation on what really matters in life. I totally believe Jesus Christ and the Bible are that foundation. The world's philosophy is to have a great time and to live it up while we are young. The problems occur when we become so deceived by the world and lose focus of our own inherent value as people. Because we all are different, we will never please every person we meet.

There are many forms of deception in life, and alcohol and drugs are one form of it. If you are not happy with who you are, don't expect to find the answer in some substance. Man will search and try many things to put in his soul, thinking he can make it better. He will always deceive himself, but he will keep on searching. You will not find peace in your heart if you conform to peer pressure. You are special, and you were accepted in God's eyes when you were conceived. Isaiah 49:1 says, "The Lord has called Me from the womb; from the bowels of my mother He has made mention of My name." God knew you by name before you were born. The Bible says you were fearfully and wonderfully made.

THE FLESH OF MAN: HIS IDOLS AND HIS GOD

The first commandment God gave man is, "You shall have no other gods before Me" (Exodus 20:3). Through knowledge, man could see the world differently. Does knowledge help you to see God, or does it lead you to believe you are your own god? If man cannot reach God his way, he will create his own god. Man has deliberately and intentionally removed God from his life. However, he cannot remove the soul God placed in each and every person. What kind of god are you putting in your heart to fill your soul?

The Bible says in Ezekiel 28:2 that through man's pride, he wants to be God. Have you turned to other things in your life to be your god? Leviticus 26:1 says, "You shall not make idols or graven images for yourselves." God wants to be first in your life, and anything you put before Him is an idol to you. Do you idolize movie stars, musicians, sports stars, the wealthy, or famous people? What are you driven by—is it success, attention, hobbies, or pleasure? What do you put first in your life?

Whatever we put in our hearts in place of God will never satisfy us. We read in Deuteronomy 7:25 that idols will become a snare to us, and they will not make us happy. The Bible tells us in Deuteronomy 4:28 that idols are "the works of men's hands, wood and stone." We created it, and we will serve it. We read in Isaiah 45:16 that everyone who makes idols will be confused.

Do the things you put before God see? Do they hear, and do they know? Jeremiah 2:28 asks if our idols save us from the stress of everyday life. Man holds onto his gods because he is trying to find meaning in life. The Bible says in Psalm 135:18 that people who have idols become like their idols. You become what you create. Man will put anything into his heart and soul, thinking he can find the answers to life. The Bible says in Jeremiah 16:14 that the day is coming in which man will say God does not exist. Has that day already come? What are you trying to put in your soul that seems satisfying on the outside but becomes empty on the inside?

THE FLESH OF MAN: SELFISHNESS

Selfishness is part of our nature from the time we are born; we seek to satisfy our needs. In Ephesians 5:29, we read that no person hates his own flesh. What about the other areas in our lives—do we look for opportunities to help others? The Bible tells us in Isaiah 43:7 that we were created for God's glory. But Isaiah 53:6 tells us man has gone astray, each one to his own way. The Bible says in 1 Corinthians 10:24, "Let no one seek his own." What does it mean to be selfish? *The American Heritage Dictionary of the English Language* defines selfishness as being concerned about oneself without regard for the well-being of others, egotistic.

I see the projection of self in all areas of life today. Most everyone wants to take a picture of themselves with their cell phones. There is a magazine in circulation called *Self*. In all sports and at all ages, if someone does something extra, they want the spotlight. Look at me; see what "I" did. Most of the time, that person never recognizes someone else who may have given them the opportunity to accomplish that feat. I believe most people who commit mass murders are doing it seeking attention. Some people will seek any means to attain it. This world's philosophy has deceived mankind. He does not know how special he is to God.

Progress and technology have affected man in how he thinks today. Man is more isolated in today's world than when I grew up as a child. Supposedly, man has more time now because of computers and cell phones; however, technology takes our time. People will text others when they are maybe just a few feet away. Many people no longer know their neighbors. When I grew up in rural America, my neighbor may have lived two to three miles away. Progress has given us technology, but it has also given us isolation. It has separated us from the people we used to turn to for social, spiritual, emotional, and physical needs. We gained technology and more time for self. In the process, however, we gave away the little things in life that brought us together.

Jesus tells us in John 7:18, "He who speaks from himself seeks his own glory." John 12:43 tells us man loves the praises of man more than the praises of God. Paul tells us in Philippians 2:21 that every person seeks his own way. The world's philosophy is to seek all the glory and pleasure you can in life and take care of yourself. If you seek your own glory, you will not please God. The Bible says in 2 Timothy 3:2, "Men will be lovers of themselves." How far will man travel in sin trying to satisfy his selfish desires? As he isolates himself more and more from the world, he becomes more selfish. As he travels down that road alone, is he finding hope or only despair? The Bible tells us in Ephesians 5:28 that husbands are to love their wives as they love their own bodies. God wants us to care about others more than we care about ourselves.

As man becomes obsessed with self, he only sees what brings self-gratification. Have we come to the point that we say, "Look what I have done"? Do we want to boast or brag to others about ourselves? The Bible tells us in Psalm 94:4, "The workers of iniquity boast in themselves." We read in Proverbs 27:1, "Do not boast about tomorrow, for you do not know what a day may bring forth." Man will boast and say he is better than someone else. You may be seeking praise and glory from man, but is it enough to satisfy your ego?

Satan and the world tell man to be number one and to look out for himself. Feed the desires of the self; don't be concerned about other people. You only have one life to live; take everything you can get to feed your empty soul; however, you will not take anything with you to your grave. The Bible tells us to love our bodies, but we are to put God first in our lives. Furthermore, we are to prefer others before ourselves. Paul tells us in 1 Corinthians 6:13 that the body is for the Lord. Every person has needs, but selfish desires will not satisfy the hunger we feel in our hearts and souls.

THE FLESH OF MAN: VANITY AND FOLLY

In writing the books of Proverbs and Ecclesiastes, Solomon uses the word *vanity* often in describing man. Solomon is noted in the Bible as someone with great knowledge and wisdom. In 1 Kings 3:9, he asks God for an understanding heart to guide Israel as their king. God granted him wisdom first and then everything else man could desire. We can learn great truths and wisdom about life from reading these books. What does vanity mean to you? *The American Heritage Dictionary of the English Language* defines vanity as a lack of usefulness, worth, or effect. It further says it is someone who is hollow, worthless, and empty. Folly is often used as well in describing man. The dictionary defines folly as the quality of being foolish, a lack of good sense and understanding. Immoral, criminal, wicked, and evil are other terms used to describe folly. Why would someone with great knowledge and wisdom use the words vanity and folly to describe mankind? Man claims to be intelligent, and he is encouraged to get an education. Knowledge, however, is empty if you do not know Jesus Christ. How much time each day do you spend on foolish, empty thoughts that do not affect you in any positive way? Do you dwell on important things in your life or on foolishness? When God breathed the breath of life into man, he became a living soul. He became a rational, thinking human being. Therefore, man is continually thinking about something all the time.

The Bible says in Psalm 94:11, "The LORD knows the thoughts of man, that they are futile." Solomon tells us in Proverbs 12:11, "He who follows frivolity is void of understanding." When man is deceived, he will trust in vanity. We read further in Proverbs 15:21, "Folly is joy to him who is destitute of discernment." Do you listen to vain people? Jeremiah 7:24 says that man walks in the counsels and the imagination of his evil heart. Do you follow your heart in the decisions of life? Jeremiah 17:9 tells us, "The heart is deceitful above all things, and desperately wicked; who can know it?" From the heart is where all of man's thoughts dwell. The Bible tells us in Genesis 6:5–7 that God saw that the wickedness of man was great in the earth and every imagination of the thoughts of his heart was continually on evil. And the Lord was sorry that He had made man. So the Lord said, "I will destroy man whom I have created from the face of the earth" (6:7). Eight people, along with the male and female of all animal life, were saved from God's judgment.

What are your goals to achieve in life? Solomon gives us a good description of what man will try to attain in the book of Ecclesiastes. In chapter 2, verses 1 through 24, we read that whatsoever Solomon desired with his eyes and heart, he set his mind to do. He pursued pleasure, laughter, and wine; he built great works; he planted vineyards and gardens; he had fountains and pools of water; he had servants; he had cattle more than anyone; he had great wealth and possessions; he had music and singers; and he had anything his heart desired. Furthermore, 1 Kings 11:3 tells us he had seven hundred wives and three hundred concubines. When he reflected back on life in Ecclesiastes 2:23, he said, "For all his days are sorrowful, and his work burdensome; even in the night his heart takes no rest." He found everything he had and did was vanity. He found emptiness, not satisfaction, in life. There was no peace, only grief and sorrow. In Ecclesiastes 12:13, Solomon sums up his life by saying, "Fear God and keep His commandments, for this is man's all."

There is guidance from God and the Bible, but people have not changed from the beginning. In Proverbs 5:23, we read that man will die for lack of instruction, and in the greatness of his folly, he shall go astray. The Bible says in Psalm 144:4, "Man is like a breath; his days are like a passing shadow." Ephesians 4:17 tells us man walks in the vanity of his heart and mind. He desires to have things his soul tells him are wrong. In Romans 8:6–8, the Bible tells us that to be carnally minded is enmity with God. James 1:8 says a double-minded person is unstable in all his ways.

What, then, do you allow to dominate your thoughts and life? Are your thoughts focused on pleasure, work, family, self, or lust? The Bible tells us God destroyed the world with a flood because every imagination of the heart was continually on evil. Paul tells us in 1 Corinthians 3:20, "The Lord knows the thoughts of the wise, that they are futile." Do you have a lot of vain, empty thoughts that have no purpose or meaning in life? Do you spend a lot of time daydreaming or wishful thinking about some fantasy where there are no problems in life? Your heart and mind can take you anywhere at any time. Only Jesus Christ can fill your heart and mind with purpose. Everything else you put there is folly and vanity.

THE FLESH OF MAN: HUNGRY AND UNSATISFIED

In the depths of man's vain mind, he is far away from the reality of life's problems. Is he seeking answers to his problems or trying to escape from them? Solomon tells us in Ecclesiastes 4:8 that he labored to be rich and found riches do not satisfy. In Ecclesiastes 7:25, we read that he applied his heart to search and know the reason for all things and found foolishness and madness. Hosea 4:10 tells us that man will eat but not have enough; he will commit all types of sexual immorality and not be satisfied. The Bible says in Isaiah 55:2 that man will spend his money for that which is not bread, and he will labor for things which do not satisfy. Solomon tells us in Proverbs 13:25, "The stomach of the wicked shall be in want." Man, of his own knowledge, does not know how to fill his empty soul.

By searching, is man trying to find the answers to life? The Bible tells us in Ecclesiastes 8:17 that man cannot find out the work that is done under the sun. For though a man labors to find it, yet he will not find it. Man will always seek to know even though he will never find the answer. The Bible tells us in Psalm 84:2 our souls long for God: "My heart and flesh cry out for the living God." There is a reason man will hunger and thirst for things to fill the emptiness in his heart. Man will always search, but he will never find the answers to life. The soul of man came from God. People can search all their lives and never find the answer in their own knowledge. Are you searching for something to put there? Are you hungry and unsatisfied?

THE FLESH OF MAN: MALE AND FEMALE, MARRIAGE

We live in a time where there are no standards, and you always have to be politically correct. The Bible says in Judges 21:25, "In those days there was no king in Israel; everyone did what was right in his own eyes." Regardless of this world's philosophy of life, we read in Genesis 1:27, "So God created man in His own image; in the image of God He created him; male and female He created them." When we are born, our birth certificates record us as male or female. There is no other category listed on that official document. The Bible tells us God's law is our schoolmaster; however, man wants to redefine God's law to justify his lifestyle.

God created all humans male and female. When Noah placed animals on the ark, God instructed him to take male and female of each species to preserve all life. The Bible says in Genesis 7:16, "Those that entered, male and female of all flesh, went in as God commanded him." In Genesis 1:28, we read that God blessed Adam and Eve and told them to "be fruitful and multiply" and replenish the earth. God's plan for man involved opposite sexes procreating to sustain life. You can remove God from how you live. Furthermore, you can call yourself transgender, or you may be a female or male couple. Life, however, can only come forth by males and females procreating together.

God created the family. The Bible says in Genesis 2:18, "It is not good that man should be alone; I will make him a helper" (some versions use "helpmate" or "help meet"). If you define each word, you find someone who helps and gives assistance to another. They contribute, help, or promote another person. They also improve, benefit, or succor someone else. "Meet" means to contend effectively with someone, to come into conformity with the views, wishes, and opinions of another and to satisfy demands, obligations, and fulfill a need of another.[47]

God created men and women different, both physically and emotionally. Alone, neither sex can fulfill all the needs of the other, whether we are male or female. God did not pick a help meet for Adam randomly. Just as God formed man from the dust of the ground, He precisely designed Eve to be the perfect help meet for Adam. God created marriage, knowing Adam and Eve's unique assets and differences. He then placed the perfect help meet for each of them. The Bible says in 1 Corinthians 7:4, "The wife does not have authority over her own body, but the husband does. And likewise, the husband does not have power over his own body, but the wife does." In God's plan for marriage, your spouse's needs are preferred before your needs. What does marriage mean to you? Is it okay for women to marry women and men to marry men? By God's standards, a woman cannot be a help meet to another woman, nor can a man be a help meet to another man. To put it bluntly, in the eyes of God, it is "impossible."

Do you accept today's worldview of marriage? Are you open-minded enough to hear what the Bible has to say about marriage? Marriage is an intimate personal union in which a man and woman consent, consummate,

---

[47] "Meet," *The American Heritage Dictionary of the English Language.*

and continually nourish a lifelong committed partnership of mutual love.[48] Marriage was created by God in the beginning when He made us male and female (Matthew 19:4). Each person was made for the other, with their natures complementary, and brought oneness into the marriage relationship (Genesis 2:24 and Matthew 19:5–6). You may ask, "How can two different people become one in marriage?" Paul tells us in 1 Corinthians 12:13 that by one Spirit, we are all baptized into one body, that body being Jesus Christ. Every believer comes to Christ through one Spirit and becomes one in Christ.

Marriage was intended to be the only way to have children and a family. Society's values are broken because the home is broken. In 2022, 23 percent of all children lived in single-parent homes.[49] Most people do not seek God before choosing a marriage partner. God tells the Jewish people to not marry unbelievers, for they will turn their hearts away from following Him (Deuteronomy 7:3–4). Paul tells us in 2 Corinthians 6:14, "Do not be unequally yoked together with unbelievers. For what fellowship has righteousness with unrighteousness?" Throughout the Bible, God warned believers to not mix with unbelievers, for they will become a snare to living a godly life. Man thinks he can mingle in sin and not suffer any consequences. Man does not want God to tell him how to live. Disobedience to God has caused most of the broken families and homes in our world today. In Matthew 19:7–9, the Pharisees came to Jesus asking Him why Moses allowed the Jews to get a divorce. Jesus told them, "Moses, because of the hardness of your hearts, permitted you to divorce your wives, but from the beginning it was not so." Jesus further says, "Whoever divorces his wife, except for sexual immorality, and marries another, commits adultery; and whoever marries her who is divorced commits adultery." God created marriage between a man and a woman to last until one spouse dies.

Christian marriages are distinct in that a man and woman covenant

---

[48] "Marriage," *Pictorial Bible Dictionary.*

[49] "National Single Parent Day: March 21, 2023," *The US Census Bureau*, March 21, 2023, https://www.census.gov/newsroom/stories/single-parent-day.html.

together with God and public witnesses to commit themselves together and to God. In unity, they seek to follow God's plan for their lives. Man can have meaningful relationships and marry, whereas, in all other forms of life, they mate with the opposite sex. Marriage requires a commitment, and that is probably why so many people prefer to live together. But even in living together as man and woman, male and female seek the other to fulfill that which is lacking in their lives. God created us male and female, knowing each of us was incomplete within our own selves. Through marriage, we can have that which we lack and need.

The Bible tells us how to live when we are married to unbelieving spouses. The unbelieving spouse can become sanctified through the believing partner if they choose to stay together (1 Corinthians 7:14). Divorce is never the first option in God's plan for marriage, even when we choose to disobey His laws.

If marriage is to be between a man and a woman, why does man want to marry someone of the same sex? With every law God has given man to direct his steps, the Bible tells of people who choose to live their lives by their own rules. The Bible says in Romans 1:26-27, "Women exchanged the natural use for what is against nature," and the men have left the natural use of the woman for another man doing that which is shameful. Paul says in 2 Timothy 3:1–3 that in the last days, men will be lovers of themselves, proud, disobedient to parents, unloving, without self-control, and despisers of that which is good. God's Word tells us that man will not find completeness in being with someone of the same sex. God created and formed the perfect help meet for each of us. It is found in someone of the opposite sex, not the same sex.

The world's philosophy of life will present many types of relationships. Each one will justify man's desire to change God's sacred meaning of marriage. What is the basis of your beliefs about marriage? The Bible tells us what marriage is, and it tells us who to look for in a lasting relationship. In a decision that is so important in life, do you want to make it alone or with God's help?

THE FLESH OF MAN: MONEY AND PLEASURE

Money and pleasure are often linked together. Most people seek some form of pleasure in life. The dictionary defines pleasure as an enjoyable sensation or emotion that brings delight or satisfaction; it is sensual gratification.[50] Man needs some form of relaxation because his life is stressful. There is nothing wrong with pleasure until it consumes your life. Relationships and the people we encounter in life are much more important than any event in which we have no control. How much do you allow pleasure from things and other people to determine how happy you are in life?

The Bible says in Proverbs 21:17 that he who loves pleasure will be poor. In Ecclesiastes 2:1 we find that Solomon looked to enjoy pleasure and found it was vanity. The Bible says in in Romans 1:32 that man takes pleasure in committing sin (KJV). Solomon tells us in Proverbs 10:23 that doing evil is a sport to a fool. In 1 Timothy 5:6, the Bible says if your life is consumed with pleasure, you are dead while you live. In the last days, man will be lovers of pleasure more than of God. James 5:5 says man lives in pleasure on earth and still wants; he has fed his desires to an insatiable heart. You can fill your life with pleasure, but your soul will be empty. Man deceives himself into thinking sin can satisfy his hungry soul. He takes pleasure in living a life in which his appetite is never full.

The Bible also tells us a lot about the evils of wealth and money. We read in 1 Timothy 6:10 that the love of money is the root of all evil. The Bible does not say "money" is the root of all evil; it says the "love of it" is the root of all evil. Anything you place before God will separate you from Him. Man equates money and wealth with being successful and having power. Jesus asks us in Luke 9:25, "What profit is it to a man if he gains the whole world, and is himself destroyed or lost?" Jesus tells us in Luke 12:34, "For where your treasure is, there your heart will be also." What do you treasure in life? Does it determine how you live?

The Bible tells us in Psalm 49:6–7 that those who trust in their wealth

---

[50] "Pleasure," *The American Heritage Dictionary of the English Language.*

and boast themselves in their riches cannot by any means redeem their brother or give a ransom to God for him. We read in Zephaniah 1:18 that silver and gold will not be able to deliver us from God's wrath nor will it satisfy our souls. Today, man desires to attain wealth, thinking it will answer every need in life. He does not realize it will not buy his way to the presence of God. Solomon tells us in Proverbs 11:28 that he who trusts in his riches will fall. Ecclesiastes 4:8 warns that if our goal in life is to become rich, we will not be satisfied with riches. Furthermore, we read in 1 Timothy 6:9 that those who desire to be rich will fall into temptation and be drawn into many foolish and hurtful lusts. The end result will be that we will drown in destruction and misery. Covetousness will only lead to sorrow in life, not happiness.

Money and wealth will not keep us from the kingdom of God. But man too often relies on his money, not God, in life. When man is full, he says he does not need God. Jesus tells us in Matthew 19:24, "It is easier for a camel to go through the eye of a needle than for a rich man to enter the kingdom of God." But in verse 26, He says, "With God all things are possible." God created all things good; there is nothing wrong with anything we have. The problem is where our priorities lie. Jesus tells us in Matthew 6:33, "But seek first the kingdom of God and His righteousness, and all these things shall be added to you." If we love God and put Him first in our lives, nothing—money, wealth, or anything else—will separate us from Him. The Bible does not tell us money, wealth, and pleasure are wrong. Rather, Paul tells us in 1 Corinthians 2:9, "Eye has not seen, nor ear heard, nor have entered into the heart of man the things which God has prepared for those who love Him." I believe God would abundantly bless His people more than we could ever realize *if* we would put Him first in everything we do.

THE FLESH OF MAN: MURDER

The sixth commandment God gave to the Jewish people said, "You shall not kill" (Exodus 20:13). In all civilized countries of the world, we are not to murder another person. In 2022, there were 6.3 murders per 100,000 people in the United States.[51] Every day, people are murdered, and often there is some form of mass murder. Many people feel guns are a problem in the world; however, there are multiple sources for a person to use if he wants to kill someone. Politicians often look at the object used as the problem. They never consider looking at man's heart. If they did, they would have to look within themselves. In Genesis 4:8, Cain slew his brother Abel. There was no gun at the time, but someone died. Man knows the problem, but it is always easier to blame a behavior on an object or his environment rather than the source of the issue. It has been said many times that the heart of the problem is man's heart.

Why do you think God said for man to not kill another person? I believe of all of God's creation, man is His crowning glory. When God formed man from the dust of the earth, he became a living soul. Man is different from anything else He created. Human life is special to God. Life came from a living source. The Bible says in Genesis 9:6, "Whoever sheds man's blood, by man his blood shall be shed; for in the image of God He made man." Why does man kill? Does he hate people? Jesus tells us in Matthew 5:22, "Whoever is angry with his brother without a cause shall be in danger of the judgment." If you let hate fester in your heart, it will destroy you before it will hurt anyone else.

THE FLESH OF MAN: ABORTION

You might ask why I would list abortion in the same area as murder, as it is a legally accepted practice in many areas of the world. I have already written about the sanctity of life. First of all, abortion is not new to man's lifestyle. Man's way of doing things may change in time, but man's heart has never changed. Furthermore, man does not learn, and that is why sin never changes.

---

[51] Ames Grawert, "Analyzing the FBI's National Crime Data on 2022—With an Eye Toward 2023 Trends," *Brennan Center for Justice*, October 18, 2023, https://www.brennancenter.org/our-work/analysis-opinion/analyzing-fbis-national-crime-data-2022-eye-toward-2023-trends.

When the Jewish people were traveling to their Promised Land, God warned them about the type of people they would encounter. God tells them in Deuteronomy 18:9-10, "When you come into the land which the Lord your God is giving you, you shall not learn to follow the abominations of those nations. There shall not be found among you anyone who makes his son or his daughter pass through the fire, or one who practices witchcraft." The term "passing through the fire" is mild language to say they burned their children to death in sacrificing them to their idols. After Israel and Judah became two different nations, the Bible tells us in 2 Kings 16:3 that the king of Israel made his son pass through the fire according to the abominations of the heathen nations. We read in Psalm 106:37 that they sacrificed their sons and daughters to demons. The Bible says in Ezekiel 16:20–21, "You took your sons and daughters, whom you bore to Me, and these you sacrificed to them to be devoured. Were your acts of harlotry a small matter, that you have slain My children and offered them up to them by causing them to pass through the fire?" God tells them, "You have slain My children." I believe there is little difference between sacrificing your children before they are born and sacrificing them after. They sacrificed their children to their gods, and today, we sacrifice our children to our gods of self.

I believe because God formed man, that is why life is so special. I know that every person is different from anyone who has ever existed. The Bible says in Psalm 139:15, "My frame was not hidden from You, when I was made in secret." God was there when I was conceived. We read in Isaiah 49:1, "The Lord has called Me from the womb . . . from the matrix of My mother He has made mention of My name." Before you were given a name by your parents, you were known by God. God brought you and me into this world; our parents were the means He used to bring us forth.

Man is very precious in the eyes of God. He knows before we do when life is to begin. If you read the Bible, you will know human life is from God; we did not evolve. As much as murder and abortion are factors in the life we live, there is a greater issue you will face. What will you do with Jesus Christ? Every issue in life comes from our heart.

THE FLESH OF MAN: STEALING

The Bible says in Exodus 20:15, "You shall not steal." This is the eighth commandment God gave to the Jewish people. Stealing is probably closely related to the tenth commandment in which God said we are not to covet. People steal because they want something they don't have, or we will steal just to destroy something that belongs to another person. We read in Leviticus 19:13, "You shall not cheat your neighbor, nor rob him." The Bible tells us in Isaiah 61:8 that God loves judgment and hates robbery. Man wants to take something from someone rather than get it legally. The FBI National Crime Data reports that the number of thefts in the US increased from 2021 to 2022: 1.0 percent for robbery, 7.4 for larceny, and 10.4 percent for motor vehicle theft.[52] Much of the crime in this country would not be a problem if the consequences followed the Bible as a guide. The Bible says in Exodus 22:1, "If a man steal an ox or a sheep, and slaughters it or sells it, he shall restore five oxen for an ox and four sheep for a sheep." With God's plan, you restore what you have taken. We read in Ecclesiastes 8:11 that because the sentence against an evil work is not executed speedily, the heart of man is fully set to do more evil. If there are little or no consequences to stealing, man will continue his evil behaviors.

Jesus tells us in John 10:10, "The thief does not come except to steal, and to kill, and to destroy. I have come that they may have life." The thief does not want to use the door; he wants to come in his way. We will only come to Jesus Christ through the door. Killing, stealing, and lying will keep us from entering the kingdom of God.

THE FLESH OF MAN: LYING

Have you ever told a lie? Maybe it was just a little lie, or maybe you said something that was not totally true. The Ten Commandments do not use the word lie explicitly; however, the ninth commandment does tell us not to bear false witness against our neighbor. The Bible says in Psalm 116:11,

---

[52] Grawert, "Analyzing the FBI's National Crime Data."

"All men are liars." The term "fake news" is commonly used in our time. Is lying the accepted behavior for man? God wants people to be truthful because He is true. Furthermore, if we lie, we are always hiding something. The Bible says in Proverbs 12:22 that lying lips are an abomination to the Lord, but the people who tell the truth are His delight. John tells us in 1 John 1:10, "If we say that we have not sinned, we make Him a liar, and His word is not in us." Psalm 78:36 says man tries to flatter God with his mouth, but he will lie with his tongue. When we lie, the only people we are deceiving are us. God knows every thought we have before any word is spoken. Are you truthful when you speak?

THE FLESH OF MAN: ABOMINATIONS

What does the word abomination mean to you? It is found in the Bible several different times. In every situation, it is used when describing a behavior of man that God abhors. *The American Heritage Dictionary of the English Language* defines abomination as something or someone disliked in a great way. It further states it is something abhorred. The dictionary defines abhor as "horror, loathing, to reject vehemently, or to shun and bring about a feeling of nausea or pungent." In Psalm 119:163, we read, "I hate and abhor lying, but I love Your law." God is holy and righteous in all His ways.

When God brought the Jewish people out of bondage, He instructed them to not be like the people who were in the land. In Deuteronomy 7:25, God tells the people to burn all the graven images and idols so they would not become a snare to them. The Bible says in Deuteronomy 27:15, "Cursed is the one who makes a carved or molded image, an abomination to the Lord." The first commandment God gave to the people said, "You shall have no other gods before Me." The second commandment said, "You shall not make for yourself any carved image."

God, not man, created Israel. He wants His people to be set apart from all other nations in the world. You may feel you can dress any way you want; however, in Deuteronomy 22:5, we read, "A woman shall not wear anything that pertains to a man, nor shall a man put on a woman's garment, for all who do so are an abomination to the LORD your God." God does not want His people to be the reason other people may become confused.

We live in a time in which men are marrying men and women are marrying women. The Bible says in Leviticus 20:13, "If a man lies with a male as he lies with a woman, both of them have committed an abomination. They shall surely be put to death." God gave man very explicit laws regarding his sexual behavior. The Bible is detailed in telling man how he is to live in all areas of life. Are you living a life that God abhors?

The Bible tells us we are not to sacrifice our children to our gods or to self. We read in Deuteronomy 12:31, "Every abomination to the Lord which He hates they have done to their gods." They have even burnt their sons and daughters to their gods. You don't see God using the word hate very often in the Bible, but some sins man commits, God calls out and tells us we better not do.

God uses the word hate again in Proverbs 6:16–19. The Bible says, "These six things the Lord hates, yes, seven are an abomination to Him: a proud look, a lying tongue, hands that shed innocent blood, a heart that devises wicked plans, feet that are swift in running to evil, a false witness who speaks lies, and one who sows discord." In Proverbs 16:5, we read, "Everyone proud in his heart is an abomination to the Lord."

In our relationships with all people, we are to be fair and just. Solomon tells us in Proverbs 11:1, "Dishonest scales are an abomination to the Lord, but a just weight is His delight." Further, in Proverbs 17:15, we read, "He who justifies the wicked, and he who condemns the just, both of them alike are an abomination to the Lord." We are to be truthful and fair in everything we do with other people.

The Bible tells us in Deuteronomy 18:9 that we are not to learn or follow the abominations of other nations. Have we gone too far against God's commandments? The Bible asks us in Jeremiah 6:15, "Were they ashamed when they had committed abomination?" No, the people were not ashamed; neither could they blush. Therefore, they shall fall among them that fall. Man likes to think God is totally a God of love and he can live any way he chooses. If you read the Bible, you will see the Jewish people, God's chosen people, were judged for their sins. All the rules are in the Bible. Are you doing anything in your life that is an abomination to Him? Am I getting too personal? I said in the beginning that the Bible will reveal to you who you really are—better than any mirror.

THE FLESH OF MAN: HIS SPEECH, HIS TONGUE

What can you say about man's tongue or his speech? The Bible says in Proverbs 18:21 that death and life are in the power of the tongue. Jesus tells us in Matthew 12:34 that man speaks from what is in his heart. If life and death are in the power of the tongue, what are we harboring in our hearts? Solomon tells us in Proverbs 13:3, "He who guards his mouth preserves his life, but he who opens wide his lips shall have destruction."

When should man speak? The Bible says in Proverbs 17:27, "He who has knowledge spares his words. And a man of understanding is of a calm spirit." In Ecclesiastes 5:3, we read that a fool's voice is known by a multitude of words. When I read these verses, I think of politicians who use a lot of words to say nothing. The book of James tells us a lot about our tongue and speech. In chapter 3, verse 2, we read that in many ways, we offend people; however, if we do not offend someone in word, we are perfect, able also to bridle the whole body. In verse 8, we read that no man can tame the tongue; it is evil and full of deadly poison. James 3:3–6 says, "We put bits in horses' mouths that they may obey us, and we turn their whole body." Also, large ships are turned by a very small rudder. But the tongue is small, and no one can control it! For it is a fire full of iniquity that defiles the whole body. In James 3 verse 10, we see, "Out of the same mouth proceed blessings and cursing," and this should not be. From the heart man speaks—what is in your heart?

All that we are comes forth through the tongue. When we speak, do we use a multitude of words to show others we are knowledgeable or a fool? The Bible says we are a perfect person if we never offend anyone with our tongue. The Bible tells us in James 1:19 that we are to be swift to hear and slow to speak. I think every person would be much wiser if he realized the tongue is a fire that no one can control.

THE FLESH OF MAN: QUICK TO SIN, JUST ONE SIN

Do you change what you believe based upon popular opinion? The Bible says in Ephesians 4:14 that we should not be like children tossed to and fro and carried about by the wind, nor should we be deceived by lies and craftiness. Jude 12 says some people are carried by the wind; they are clouds without water. Being politically correct means there is no foundation; nothing is fundamentally true. The Bible says in James 1:6 that we are not to waver, for he who wavers is like a wave of the sea driven with the wind and tossed. Are you tossed about by the world's philosophy of life? Are you prone to changing your mind often? The Bible says if you associate with people who change quickly, you will be confused.

I have heard many people say, "I am just one person, and my sin will not affect anyone." The Bible says in Romans 14:7 that no person lives to himself, and no one dies to himself. We read in Ecclesiastes 9:18 that one sinner destroys much good. Chemistry will show that one speck of dirt in a clear glass of water will make the whole glass dirty. Romans 5:12 says, "Through one man sin entered into the world, and death through sin, and thus death spread, because all sinned." You can go your own way and feel you are just one person; what difference will one sin make? Solomon says in Proverbs 28:26 that he who trusts in his own heart is a fool. We were not created to live alone. We don't realize how many people we touch in our lifetime. By the world's standards, we may feel we are nobody. But with God, we were somebody when we were conceived. From the movie *It's A Wonderful Life,* George found he touched so many lives. He thought he was a failure. We really do not realize how many people we touch in some way during our lifetime.

The Flesh of Man: Blaming Others—It's Not Your Fault

We live in a time in which we have no-fault insurance and claim we are victims of society. We may feel the problems we are incurring in life are from our environment and not from the choices we made. Jeremiah 10:23 says, "The way of man is not in himself; it is not in man who walks to direct his own steps." Every person makes many decisions every day, never thinking about the consequences of those choices. We have heard it said many times that life is not fair. The Bible says in Proverbs 1:31 that we will eat the fruit of our own ways, and we will be filled with our own devices. We will reap what we sow. Deception will not be an excuse; people are led, never driven. In Deuteronomy 24:16, the Bible says, "Fathers shall not be put to death for their children, nor shall children be put to death for their fathers; a person shall be put to death for his own sin." You may feel life has been unfair to you, but every person will stand before God alone for the choices he made in life. The Bible tells us in Romans 14:12 that every person will give an account of himself to God. The Bible says in Matthew 9:4 that God knows our thoughts, and He knows the intent of our hearts. Is your life going the direction you want? If not, whose fault is it?

The Flesh of Man: Living in the Valley of Decision

From the beginning, Adam and Eve made a decision that affected their lives and all mankind. They chose to believe Satan's lie rather than believe God. The Bible says in Deuteronomy 28:1–68 that God gave the Jewish people a choice before they settled in Canaan: blessings or a curse. In Joshua 24:15, he tells the people, "Choose for yourselves this day whom you will serve, whether the gods which your fathers served that *were* on the other side of the River, or the gods of the Amorites, in whose land you dwell. But as for me and my house, we will serve the Lord." The Bible tells us there is not anyone good but God (Mark 10:18). We have a choice: be obedient to Him, and He will richly bless us; or we can live our way and suffer the consequences.

The Bible says in Joel 3:14 that there are multitudes and multitudes of people who are in the valley of decision, for the day of the Lord is near. Every day, we choose how we live. How many of those decisions affect our families and those we are around? Choice is a basic fundamental part of every person. The greatest decision we will ever make in life is what we will do with Jesus Christ. Jesus tells us in John 3:16, "God so loved the world that He gave His only begotten Son, that whoever believes in Him should not perish but have everlasting life." Jesus is always reaching out to man. Are you in the valley of decision? Judgment is coming—are you ready?

THE FLESH OF MAN: THE JUDGMENT OF GOD

Do you have a fear of the future or eternity? Jesus tells us in Matthew 10:28, " Do not fear those who kill the body but cannot kill the soul. But rather fear Him who is able to destroy both soul and body in hell." Why is it man does not fear God, but nations fear Israel? Nations know about the God of Israel. Israel was made a country again in 1948. It is about the size of New Hampshire. Even though it is small in size, all the world knows about Israel and its God.

Throughout the Bible, you will find God does not let sin go unpunished. The Bible gives us reference after reference to God's judgment against Israel for its sins. Maybe people do not fear God because they have not personally seen or felt His judgment. Every true Christian knows God chastises His people. In Ecclesiastes 11:9 we read God will bring us into judgment.

Although man does not fear God, demons fear Him. The Bible says in Matthew 8:28–29 that devils and demons know Jesus. They also know they have a short time to deceive the world. Men may say there is no God, but Roman 1:18 says God's wrath on sin is revealed against all ungodliness of men. In Acts 17:31, we read that God "has appointed a day on which He will judge the world in righteousness." Jesus tells us in John 3:18, "He who does not believe is condemned already." The Bible asks us in Hebrews 2:3, "How shall we escape if we neglect so great salvation?" Jesus Christ has offered this gift of salvation to all men.

God has been removed from our schools and in all public areas in our country. It seems man no longer thinks about God except when some disaster happens. Jesus tells us in Matthew 24:38–39, "For as in the days before the flood, they were eating and drinking, marrying and giving in marriage, until the day that Noah entered the ark, and did not know until the flood came and took them all away." Man was so wrapped up in his own world that he did not know there is a righteous God. Eight people and all male and female animal life were spared. Sin was judged, and it will be judged again by Jesus Christ. The Bible says all men will face the judgment seat of Jesus Christ. The Bible says all creation reveals God and our soul knows Him. Judgment is coming; when you die, it will be too late. Are you ready to face Jesus Christ?

QUESTIONS FOR REFLECTION

1. If we are evolving, does breaking the law make us better?
2. How does it make you feel to know God knows everything in your heart?
3. There is no darkness, and everything is in the light, open to God. Judgment is coming; are you ready?

WHO IS GOD?
THE CHARACTER
OF GOD

I am the Alpha and the Omega, the Beginning and the End.
—REVELATION 1:8

You may be asking if Jesus is God, why do I need to have two separate chapters about Him. God is, and always has been, Spirit. In eternity, He may reveal Himself to everyone in heaven. Jesus Christ is God, but He came to earth as flesh and blood so that man could know Him personally. He had a distinct character separate from God the Father. God never died, but Jesus Christ willingly died on the cross to redeem all mankind from their sins. The Holy Spirit is the third person of the Trinity. He primarily came forth when Jesus ascended to heaven, and He lives in all Christians. Although Jesus is God, His character is different in many ways in the Bible. That is the reason I want to try to describe God differently than Jesus Christ.

Who is God, and what is His character? Is man his own god? Satan wanted to be equal to or higher than God. He was thrown out of heaven with one-third of the angels. Then, who is God, and where did He come from? There is no way my earthly mind can fully describe God. What I do know about Him, the Holy Spirit and the Bible have revealed to me.

GOD IS OMNIPRESENT, OMNIPOTENT, OMNISCIENT

God is infinite, and He is everywhere. The Bible says in Lamentations 5:19 that God is eternal: "You, O LORD, remain forever." Even though God is Spirit, He lives. In 1 Samuel 17:26, David says that man should not defy the armies of the living God. Jesus says in John 6:51, "I am the living bread which came down from heaven." Revelation 1:8 says, "I am the Alpha and the Omega, the Beginning and the End."

God told Moses in Exodus 33:20, "You cannot see My face; for no man shall see Me and live." In John 1:18, the Bible tells us no man has seen God at any time. Paul tells us in 1 Timothy 1:17 that God the King is eternal, immortal, and invisible. In 1 Timothy 6:16, we read that God dwells in immortality in the light, which no man can approach and no man has seen or can see. Furthermore, the Bible says in 2 Corinthians 4:1 that the things we see are temporal, but that which we do not see is eternal. The thought that God is Spirit is something people have a problem understanding. A common saying is, "Out of sight, out of mind." Some religious leaders claim they have seen God, but the Bible says no one has ever seen God.

There is only *one* God who fills the heavens and earth. In 2 Samuel 7:22, we read, "You are great, O LORD God. For there is none like You, nor is there any God besides You." Isaiah 43:10 says, "I am He. Before Me there was no God formed, nor shall there be after Me." We read in Ephesians 4:6 that there is one God and Father of all mankind. The Bible says in 1 John 5:7, "For there are three that bear witness in heaven: the Father, the Word, and the Holy Spirit; and these three are one."

The Bible tells us God is everywhere, but man chooses not to see Him. The Bible says in Psalm 19:1, "The heavens declare the glory of God; and the firmament shows His handiwork." In Isaiah 6:3, we read, "The whole earth is full of His glory!" Everything that exists in the heavens and on earth reveals God. Omnipresence is the word used to describe that God is everywhere at all times. In Proverbs 15:3, the Bible says, "The eyes of the Lord are in every place, keeping watch on the evil and the good." In Isaiah

66:1, we read, "Heaven is My throne, and the earth is My footstool." The Bible asks us in Jeremiah 23:24, "Can anyone hide himself in secret places, so I shall not see him? Do I not fill heaven and earth?" Even though God is everywhere at all times, the Bible tells us in Acts 17:27 that if any person seeks the Lord, he will find Him because God is not far from us.

God is all-powerful and has all authority. Omnipotent is the word that is best used to describe God's unlimited power. The Bible tells us in Genesis 7 that God destroyed the world with a flood. In Exodus 14:21, God parted the Red Sea. In all things, God controls life and nature. We read in Job 42:2 that God can do everything. In Psalm 145:3, the Bible says the Lord is great, and His greatness is unsearchable. In His infinite and eternal power, all things in this world continue as He wants them to be. Man may think he can do anything he wants, but God is in total control.

God is also omniscient—He is all-knowing. Man wants to hide in the dark, thinking no one will see him. The Bible says in 2 Chronicles 6:30 that God alone knows the hearts of men. Job 34:21 says, "For His eyes are on the ways of man, and He sees all his steps." The Bible says in Daniel 2:22 that God can see the deep and secret things; He knows what is in the darkness because light dwells within Him. We see in Hebrews 4:13 that there is nothing hidden from His sight, for all things are naked and open to His eyes. How many times each day do we try to hide something from someone? In man's thinking, if no one sees what happens, no one will know. All creation is open to Him; He is all-powerful, He is present everywhere, and He is all-knowing. The Bible says in Romans 11:33, "Oh, the depth of the riches both of the wisdom and knowledge of God! How unsearchable are His judgments and His ways past finding out!"

If you are a true believer, you know God is real and dwells in your soul. I used the Bible to describe the character of God as best as I could. However, I also used *The American Heritage Dictionary of the English Language* and the *Pictorial Bible Dictionary*. In describing the character of God, I need to start from the top, and it is not love.

GOD IS HOLY

There are a lot of people who believe they can live in sin and they will go to heaven because of God's love. If you read the Bible, you will find that is not true. When you see the word "holy," what comes to your mind? Holy means to be separate and set apart from evil. It is often used with the words righteous, true, just, clean, and pure. When Moses first went to Mt. Sinai, where God dwelt, he was told, "Take your sandals off your feet, for the place where you stand is holy ground" (Exodus 3:5). When Moses was instructed to build the tabernacle, God told him in Exodus 26:33 to separate the Most Holy Place from all other areas. God gave the Jewish people laws to live by, and in Leviticus 10:10, He told them to distinguish between clean and unclean and holy and unholy. Leviticus 19:2 says, "You shall be holy, for I the LORD your God am holy."

The Bible says in Psalm 60:6 that God speaks in holiness. Bibles are called Holy Bibles. In everything, God is holy. The Bible says in Isaiah 6:3, "Holy, Holy, Holy is the LORD of hosts; the whole earth is full of His glory!" In Isaiah 43:3, we read, "For I am the LORD your God, the Holy One of Israel, your Savior." Because God is holy, He wants every person to be that way. Do you try to live up to God's standards?

In Luke 4:33–34, we see demons did not want to be around Jesus because they knew He was the Holy One of God. When Jesus was praying to God in John 17:11, He called God the "Holy Father." The Bible tells us in Romans 7:12 that God's law is holy and just and good. Everything about God is holy. The Bible says in 1 Corinthians 3:16–17 that the Holy Spirit dwells in born-again Christians. In every Christian's physical body, the temple of God dwells, and that temple is holy.

GOD IS LOVE

From the beginning, man was special to God. Man was God's crowning glory of all His creation. Most people are familiar with John 3:16, which says: "For God so loved the world that He gave His only begotten Son, that whoever believes in Him should not perish but have everlasting life." People see the first part of that verse and never see the rest of it. They see God's love, and that is all they want to see. It also says that whosoever *believes* in Jesus Christ can have everlasting life. In John 10:15, Jesus says, "I lay down My life for the sheep," which is every person who has ever existed. Jesus tells us in John 15:13, "Greater love has no one than this, than to lay down one's life for his friends." All of man's sins have been covered by the blood of Jesus Christ.

The Bible tells us in Psalm 26:3 that God's lovingkindness is before our eyes. In Jeremiah 31:3, we read that God has always loved us with an everlasting love. Even though man may choose not to believe in God, we cannot get away from His love. The Bible asks in Romans 8:35, "Who shall separate us from the love of Christ? Shall tribulation, or distress, or persecution, or famine, or nakedness, or peril, or sword?" Paul continues in Romans 8:38–39: "Neither death nor life, nor angels nor principalities nor powers, nor things present nor things to come, nor height nor depth, nor any other created thing, shall be able to separate us from the love of God which is in Christ Jesus our Lord." There is nothing we can do or anything we have to do to earn the love of Christ. It reaches to the deepest, darkest parts of the world and into the most secret places in the hearts of men.

Man's love changes with time and the circumstances of life. The Bible tells us the source of real love is not in man. 1 John 4:7 says, "Love is of God." In verse 10, we read that man did not choose to love God, but God chose to love us and sent His Son to die for our sins. Man can love because God first loved us (1 John 4:19). There are many, many people who feel God does not love them. Every person needs to understand that God will judge man's sin; however, Jesus Christ died for the sinner. That includes every person who has ever existed. God hates sin, but He loves people. God can separate man's nature from his soul. Most people, including me, have a problem separating the sin from the person. Jesus Christ died for every person, and you are loved whether you feel it or not.

What is the character of real love? The Bible tells us in 1 Corinthians 13 what true love should be. You may be an eloquent speaker, have great knowledge and wisdom, and give to all kinds of charities, but if you do not have love in your heart, it is meaningless. Love is patient; it is kind. It does not envy anyone or anything, and it is not puffed up. It does not provoke or seek its own. It does not rejoice in iniquity but in truth. It bears all things; it believes, hopes, and endures all things. Love never fails because it gives. Love is perfect. The greatest gift man can have is to have love for other people.

Romans 13:10 tells us love does not cause ill feelings with anyone; it fulfills the law. In Ephesians 3:17, we read that if Christ dwells in our hearts, we should be rooted and grounded in love. Furthermore, Ephesians 5:2 says we should walk in love as Christ has loved us and has given Himself for us. If we are Christians, love is not an option. It should be something that dwells in our hearts and flows through us.

GOD IS RIGHTEOUS

What does righteousness mean to you? It means to do things right or to make right. The Bible says in Deuteronomy 4:8 that all of God's law is righteous. Psalm 9:8 says God will judge the world in righteousness. The Bible tells us in Psalm 45:7 that God loves righteousness and hates wickedness. In Psalm 97:2, we read that God lives in the midst of judgment and righteousness. Solomon tells us in Proverbs 14:34, "Righteousness exalts a nation, but sin is a reproach to any people." Daniel 9:7 says, "O LORD, righteousness belongs to You, but to us shame of face." The Bible says in 2 Corinthians 5:21 that Christ, who knew no sin, was made sin for us that we might become the righteousness of God in Him. God loves righteousness and hates iniquity. Are you living righteous before others? God commands us to love others and live righteously.

GOD IS PURE

If something is pure, it has to be full strength; it cannot be mixed. It has to be totally clear, sinless, and perfect. Have you ever looked at something and saw that it was crystal clear? Jesus Christ is pure and perfect. He had to be to meet God's demands for the blood sacrifice to cover all of man's sins. Do you have any concept of what purity means? The Bible asks in Job 4:17, "Can a mortal be more righteous than God? Can a man be more pure than his maker?" Can something created be better than the Creator of all things? In Psalm 12:6, we read, The words of the Lord are pure words, like silver tried in a furnace of earth, purified seven times." Psalm 119:140 says God's Word is very pure. Solomon tells us in Proverbs 30:5, "Every word of God is pure; He is a shield to those who put their trust in Him."

Micah 6:11 tells us people claim to be pure by using wicked scales and deceit as guidelines. The only way anyone can be pure is by following God's Word, the Bible. We read in Philippians 4:8 that whatsoever things are true, honest, just, pure, of good report, and of any other virtue, we should think on these things. James 3:17 says, "The wisdom that is from above is first pure, then peaceable, gentle, willing to yield, full of mercy and good fruits, without partiality and without hypocrisy."

GOD IS TRUTH

Truth has been written about already when telling about the different roles Christ lived before all mankind. However, Isaiah 16:5 tells us God's throne is established in truth. In Jeremiah 4:2, we read that the Lord lives in truth, judgment, and righteousness. The Bible says in Hebrews 6:18 that it is impossible for God to lie. We read in Titus 1:2 that the hope of eternal life is in God, who cannot lie. Are you confused and do not know what to believe? The Bible says in 1 Corinthians 14:33, "For God is not the author of confusion but of peace." Truth is a light; it is before your eyes. If you walk toward it, you will not stumble and fall.

GOD IS LIGHT

Jesus tells man to walk in the day when he can see. Without light, man cannot see in the dark. In Job 34:21, we read, "His eyes are on the ways of man, and He sees all his steps." In Psalm 104:2, the Bible says God is covered with light as a garment. In eternity, there will be no need for the sun or moon in heaven, for the glory of God will illuminate it (Revelation 21:23).

Jesus tells us in John 8:12, " I am the light of the world. He who follows Me shall not walk in darkness, but have the light of life." Jesus says in John 12:46, "Whoever believes in Me should not abide in darkness." Jesus is the source of true light; however, truth and light expose everything in man's heart. With God, there is no difference between day and night. There will be no sun in eternity, and Jesus Christ will be that light. That kind of light is why nothing is hidden from God.

The Bible tells us there are other notable characteristics of God. Colossians 3:10–14 tells us, as followers of Christ, to put on mercy, kindness, humility, meekness, patience, forgiveness, and love. Galatians 5:22–25 tells us, "The fruit of the Spirit is love, joy, peace, longsuffering, kindness, goodness, faithfulness, gentleness, and self-control." If we have the Spirit of God dwelling within us, we are to walk in the Spirit. God has a standard by which He wants man to live.

GOD IS MERCY

Mercy is helping the weak, sick, and poor. God showed mercy to all people when He sent His Son, Jesus Christ, to die on the cross for our sins. In Numbers 14:18, we read, "The Lord is longsuffering and abundant in mercy." In 1 Chronicles 16:34, the Bible says the Lord's mercy endures forever. Lamentations 3:22–23 says that it is by the Lord's mercies that we are not consumed. For they are new every morning. Micah 7:18 asks who is like God, who pardons sin and does not hold anger toward man because He delights in mercy. In Titus 3:5, we read that God's mercy is not because of any righteousness man has done. It is by His mercy He saved us and washed our sins away. God is merciful and does not want anyone to spend eternity in hell; however, God's mercy does not override every person's free will to choose.

GOD IS KIND

Kindness is described as being charitable, friendly, helpful, and with a warm heart. Nehemiah 9:17 says God is ready to pardon, slow to anger, and abundant in kindness. In Isaiah 54:8, we read that God has an everlasting kindness to man. In the second great commandment, Jesus tells us to love our neighbor as ourselves. Showing kindness to others is showing godly character.

GOD IS MEEK

Some would say that meekness is being weak. The Bible says in Numbers 12:3 that Moses was very meek above all the men who were upon the face of the earth. Meekness is defined as being humble and patient when helping others. In Psalm 37:11, the Bible says, "The meek shall inherit the earth, and shall delight themselves in the abundance of peace." The Bible tells us in 1 Timothy 6:11 that we are to live in righteousness, godliness, faith, love, patience, and meekness. Furthermore, Titus 3:2 instructs us to not speak evil of any man but to be gentle and show meekness to all men. Godly character is to be meek.

GOD IS LONGSUFFERING, PATIENT

These two words are very similar in meaning. Longsuffering means to patiently endure in difficult times. Patience means to be tolerant, calm, and enduring. It also means to bear affection toward someone with calmness. When the word longsuffering is used in the Bible, it is talking about God's relationship with man; however, patience is used when talking about man's walk with God. Most people want to do things now, our way. Man can be very impatient, yet God is longsuffering, waiting for man to come to Him. Any believer who can truly look at himself knows God is longsuffering in His relationship with us.

In Psalm 86:15, we read that the Lord God is full of compassion and grace; He is longsuffering and plentiful in mercy and truth. The Bible tells us in Romans 2:4 to not despise the riches of God's goodness, forbearance, and longsuffering; for the goodness of God leads man to repentance. In 2 Peter 3:9, the Bible says, "The Lord is not slack concerning His promise, as some count slackness, but is longsuffering toward us, not willing that any should perish but that all should come to repentance." How many people have made God wait, saying, "Not today"? The Bible tells us we may not have tomorrow. God is longsuffering and not willing that anyone should perish.

The Bible tells us in James 1:3–4 that the trying of our faith brings patience. We should let patience have its perfect work so that we may be perfect and complete, lacking nothing. We live in a time in which man has a remote control and wants to change things now. Believers know that when we pray to God, the answer is not usually immediate. The Bible says in Esther 4:14 that we will receive an answer at the time it is most needed in our life, "for such a time as this."

GOD IS FORGIVING

Forgiveness means giving up our restraint or giving requital of an offense committed against us. It is the willingness to repair and restore a relationship. When Jesus was crucified on the cross, Luke 23:34 says He asked God to forgive those people for they did not know what they had done. He forgave you and me as much as He did all those people who were there.

The Bible says in 2 Chronicles 7:14, "If My people who are called by My name will humble themselves, and pray and seek My face, and turn from their wicked ways, then I will hear from heaven, and will forgive their sin and heal their land." Psalm 86:5 says the Lord is good and ready to forgive, and He is abundant in mercy to all those who call upon Him. In

Daniel 9:9, we read, "To the Lord our God belong mercy and forgiveness, though we have rebelled against Him."

Christ has forgiven man for crucifying Him, and He will forgive us our sins if we seek Him through repentance. Jesus tells us in Matthew 6:14–15 that if we forgive men their trespasses, our heavenly Father will also forgive us. But if we do not forgive men their trespasses, neither will our Father forgive our trespasses. Paul tells us in Ephesians 4:32 that we are to be tenderhearted and forgiving to one another as God, for Christ's sake, has forgiven us. Forgiveness is an attribute of God. He reaches out to us to restore that relationship to Him that man's sin has broken. Has forgiving someone hindered your ability to repair a relationship?

GOD IS GENTLE

Gentleness is described as being kind, not harsh, easygoing, and showing meekness to all people. In Psalm 18:35, we read, "Your gentleness has made me great." Paul tells us in 2 Corinthians 10:1 that Jesus Christ is meek and gentle. James 3:17 says the wisdom we receive from God is first pure, then peaceable, gentle, willing to yield, full of mercy, without partiality and hypocrisy.

God's standard on how to live requires a high degree of love and discipline. The Bible says in 2 Timothy 2:24 that a servant of the Lord must not quarrel but be gentle to all men. Titus 3:2 tells us to not speak evil to anyone nor be a brawler but to be gentle and meek to all men. Paul says in 1 Thessalonians 2:7 that the gentleness we are to show to others is as a nursing mother who cherishes her own children. The Bible tells us that gentleness from God will make us a better person.

GOD IS GOOD

What does goodness mean to you? The Bible tells us man's goodness is as filthy rags. Goodness is described as being virtuous, moral, kind, generous, and having worth and quality. The Bible says in Exodus 34:6 that God is merciful, longsuffering, and abundant in goodness and truth. Psalm 31:19 says, "How great is Your goodness, which You have laid up for all those who fear You." Psalm 33:5 says the earth is full of the goodness of the Lord. In James 1:17, the Bible says, "Every good and perfect gift is from above." It is not for man's goodness that God is good to us.

GOD IS FAITHFUL

Hebrews 11:6 says, "Without faith it is impossible to please Him." Being faithful means being reliable, constant, loyal, dependable, and responsible. The Bible tells us in Deuteronomy 7:9 that God is faithful and keeps His promises to a thousand generations. In 1 Kings 8:56, we read, "Blessed be the Lord, who has given rest to His people Israel, according to all that He has promised. There has not failed one word of all His good promise, which He promised through His servant Moses." The Bible tells us in Hebrews 11:1 that faith is the substance of things hoped for and the evidence of things not seen. There are things in this world you believe and hold onto, yet you have never seen. What is the basis of those feelings?

GRACE: GOD'S UNMERITED LOVE TO MAN

Is grace the prayer you sometimes ask before a meal? Consider what the word grace means to you. Grace is the kindness of God bestowed upon man. All mankind receives God's universal grace, and those of us who are born again receive His saving grace. As you can see, everyone does not receive the same amount of grace in their lives. Grace might be like true light: everyone receives some of it.

The Bible says in Exodus 22:27 that God is gracious. Jonah 4:2 tells us he knew God was gracious, merciful, slow to anger, and of great kindness. In Zechariah 12:10, we read, "I will pour on the house of David and on the inhabitants of Jerusalem the Spirit of grace." John 1:16–17 tells us we all have received grace, for the law was given by Moses, but grace and truth came by Jesus Christ. The Bible says in 2 Corinthians 9:8, "God is able to make all grace abound to you, that you, always having all sufficiency in all things, may have an abundance for every good work." Jesus tells us in 2 Corinthians 12:9, "My grace is sufficient for you, for My strength is made perfect in weakness." Therefore, we are to take glory in our infirmities so that the power of Jesus Christ may rest upon us.

The Bible says in Ephesians 2:8–9, "For by grace you have been saved through faith, and that not of yourselves; it is the gift of God, not of works, lest anyone should boast." Man cannot and did not do anything to attain salvation; it is totally by the love and grace of God. It is a gift from Him. We read in Titus 2:11, "For the grace of God that brings salvation has appeared to all men." God's universal grace and love abound toward every person. You will either want it in your heart, or you will walk away from it. Every person has been invited to come. There are no hidden stipulations that keep you from His love and grace.

GOD SAVES WHOSOEVER

There are people who think their sins are so bad God would not save them. The Bible says in Deuteronomy 4:29 that if you seek the Lord God with all your heart and with all your soul, you will find Him. In Psalm 145:18, we read that the Lord is near to all who call upon Him in truth. You have to be seeking Him with your whole heart, not just wishing He would fix your problems. In Joel 2:32, the Bible says that whoever calls on the name of the Lord shall be saved. God does not put restrictions on who may come to Him. Four of the greatest people in the Bible had problems with sin. Abraham lied to the rulers in Egypt about his wife, telling them Sarah was his sister. Moses, David, and Paul killed someone or had someone killed. If you seek God with all your heart, you will find Him, whosoever may come freely.

Only God Can Change Your Heart

I know of three men in my church who experienced a total makeover of their lives by God. That makeover happened the minute they gave their hearts to Jesus Christ. *Unbroken* tells the story of Louis Zamperini. He spent forty-three days on a life raft in the Pacific Ocean after his plane crashed in WW II. He was rescued by the Japanese and spent over two years as a prisoner of war. He was tortured to near death in that camp. When the war ended, he came home with a heart full of hate and anger. His mind could not turn off the horror he had been through. Alcohol became his escape to relieve the pain he felt in his soul. He attended a Billy Graham revival in Los Angeles three to four years after the war ended. The second night he went, the Holy Spirit reached down into his heart, and he was forever changed. The hate, anger, and desire for alcohol left his heart immediately.[53]

Remarkable changes take place in man's soul when he gives his heart to Jesus Christ. How can it be that God can take a broken body and spirit and put it back together again? When Christ makes you whole, you are ready for His honor and glory.

The Bible says in Psalm 40:1–3, "I waited patiently for the Lord; and He inclined to me, and heard my cry. He also brought me up out of a horrible pit, out of the miry clay, and set my feet upon a rock, and established my steps. He has put a new song in my mouth—praise to our God." We read in Jeremiah 24:7 that God has given us a heart to know Him that we may know He is God. In Ezekiel 11:19, we read that God will give man one heart and put a new spirit within him, and He will take the stony heart out of his flesh. The Bible tells us in Zechariah 3:4 that God will take away the filthy garments from us and cause our iniquity to pass from us and clothe us with new raiment. John 1:13 says that when we are born again, we are no longer in the will of the flesh or of man but of God.

---

[53] Laura Hillenbrand, *Unbroken: A World War II Story of Survival, Resilience, and Redemption* (New York: Random House, 2014).

When we receive Christ into our hearts, we become a new person. In 2 Corinthians 5:17, the Bible says, "If anyone is in Christ, he is a new creation; old things have passed away; behold, all things have become new." That change is not from anything we can do, nor from man's righteousness, but according to God's mercy. Once we are saved, 1 Peter 1:23 says we are no longer of corruptible seed but incorruptible by the Word of God, which lives and abides forever.

The people I know changed immediately. God knows how to put all the broken pieces back together again better than before. If you are in some type of accident, surgeons will attempt to put your body back together on the outside. When God enters your life, He puts you back together, starting on the inside. He will give you a new heart. You truly will be a new creation in Christ; old things are passed away, and you become new.

GOD IS PERFECT

The Bible says in 2 Samuel 22:31, "As for God, His way is perfect." In Deuteronomy 32:4, we read that God is the Rock, and His work is perfect, for all His ways are judgment and truth without iniquity, just and right is He. Job 36:4 says God is perfect in knowledge. The Bible says in Hebrews 5:9 that being made perfect, Christ became the author of eternal salvation unto all who obey Him. Man will never be perfect; however, we can become more like Christ in the way we live.

WHEN GOD HIDES HIS FACE FROM MAN

Man thinks God is always there regardless of how he lives. It is true God loves all mankind universally. That love cost God everything, the death of His Son Jesus Christ. The Bible says in 1 Corinthians 6:20 that man has been bought with a price. God is holy and righteous. The Bible tells us there are times in which God hides His face from us. Are you aware of when that can happen? If you are a true Christian, you know sin separates us from God. The Bible tells us sin and holiness cannot cohabit at the same time in man's soul.

Psalm 66:18 says, "If I regard iniquity in my heart, the Lord will not hear." Isaiah 59:2 says, "Your iniquities have separated you from your God; and your sins have hidden His face from you, so that He will not hear." The Jewish people have suffered many heartaches throughout their history because they did not obey God.

Hosea 5:6 says that man will gather all he has and try to find God, but they will not find Him. Man does not come to God when he is full. He comes to God when he seeks Him with his whole empty heart. In Micah 3:4, we read that man will cry unto the Lord, but He will not hear them. He will hide His face from them because of their evil ways. Habakkuk 1:13 says God has pure eyes to see evil and cannot look on sin. God does not look upon sin, and that is why Jesus Christ is the focal point throughout the Bible. From the foundations of the world, Jesus Christ is our Mediator to God. True believers come to God by the sinless blood of Jesus Christ. God sees Christ's blood, not our sins.

CHASTISEMENT

What comes to your mind when you hear the word chastisement? Chastisement is defined as punishment, instruction, training, and discipline. From an early age, children learn to be disobedient to their parents. If you punish your children in public, some people think you are abusing them. You may also get a visit from social services. There are people who believe the Bible tells us to beat our children with a rod. They may be using Proverbs 23:13 as the basis of their beliefs, which says, "Do not withhold correction from a child, for if you beat him with the rod, he will not die." It is interesting that society will take one verse to judge God and the Bible about disciplining children; however, they will never know true love until they know God. They see the word *beat* but cannot see the word *love*. There are 76 times in the Bible where the word beat or beaten is used. But there are 408 times in which the word love or loved is used. People see only what they want to see. Discipline and love go together; they are not two totally separate feelings and actions of man.

I see children now who are warned to stop doing something, yet there is no consequence for continued bad behavior. Parents may not know how to discipline their children, or they may fear the judgment of other people. Has the world's view of chastisement changed to where it is no longer politically correct to discipline children?

I also spent almost four years in the military during the Vietnam War. The first thing you learn is discipline; you learn real quick to obey orders. Discipline and following rules are a fundamental part of the military and life. Everyone cannot go in different directions in life and expect to reach the same goal. Man can see the verse in the Bible about beating their children with a rod. But he is totally blind in not seeing something far greater, the love of God.

In every area of life, the Bible has a plan for man. So what can we learn from the Bible about chastisement? In Deuteronomy 8:5, we read, "As a man chastens his son, so the LORD your God chastens you." Job 5:17 says, "Happy is the man whom God corrects; therefore do not despise the chastening of the Almighty." Job 23:10 tells us God knows the way we are going, and He will direct our steps. We shall come forth as gold refined in the furnace. Solomon says in Proverbs 3:11–12, "My son, do not despise the chastening of the Lord, nor detest His correction; for whom the Lord loves He corrects." We discipline our children because we love them, not to abuse them. The Bible tells us in Malachi 3:3 that as a refiner purifies silver, God will purify believers as gold and silver that they may offer unto God righteousness.

In 2 Timothy 3:16, we read that the Bible is profitable to man for doctrine, for reproof, for correction, and for instruction in righteousness. Hebrews 12:6 tells us that everyone the Lord loves He will chasten, and in verses 7 through 10, we find that if we endure chastening, we are sons of God. We endure chastisement by our parents and give them respect. Our parents can discipline us for many different reasons, but God does it for our benefit so that we may be partakers of His holiness. The Bible says in Hebrews 12:11, "Now no chastening seems to be joyful for the present, but painful; nevertheless, afterward it yields the peaceable fruit of righteousness to those who have been trained by it." We see in 1 Peter 1:7 that the trial of our faith is much more precious than gold that will perish when tried in the fire.

GOD ALWAYS WARNS MAN

If you see or hear a warning, what do you do? Do you ignore it, wish it would go away, or do you take heed and follow the directions to safety? Warnings are given to make people aware of danger. The Bible is filled with warnings to man to repent of his sins, believe in Jesus Christ, and spend eternity with God; however, man chooses to go his own way in life and not believe God. He deliberately chooses to disregard what the Bible says. If you die today, eternity starts today—are you ready?

Paul says in 1 Corinthians 4:14 that God has given man the Bible not to shame us but as sons to warn us. God warned His people Israel to be obedient to His commandments or face the consequences of their behaviors. If you know anything about the Jewish people, you know they endured great suffering. God did not ignore the sins of the nation He created. Sin costs much more than you and I want to pay. The Bible gives man plenty of warning of the consequences of choosing a life apart from Him.

There is a day coming in which this world as we know it will end. Satan exalts himself against everything of God. He is the father of lies and the great deceiver to all mankind. The Bible says in Jeremiah 6:10, "To whom shall I speak and give warning, that they may hear?" They hear, but they do not understand; God's Word is a reproach to them, and they do not want to listen. In Ezekiel 33:5, we read, "He heard the sound of the trumpet, but did not heed the warning; his blood shall be upon himself. But he who takes the warning will save his life." Paul tells us in Colossians 1:28 that every person is warned through the preaching of the gospel. The warning has been sounded, and every person can know if he will read the Bible.

The Bible says God does not lie. From the beginning, men have known to obey God or suffer the consequences of their sins. The Bible is a guide to joy and eternal life, but it is filled with warnings about living a life apart from God. It is God's desire that no one spend eternity in hell. Salvation is free; there is nothing we can do to earn or buy it. God told the Jewish people in Deuteronomy 11:26, "Behold, I set before you this day a blessing and a curse." The warning has been sounded; you will choose whom you will serve.

GOD IS NO RESPECTER OF PERSONS

There are no classes of people with God, nor are there different races or nationalities. We all come to Christ the same way, humbly as children. God does not place one person above another. In Psalm 98:9, we read that the Lord will judge the earth with righteousness and equity. God will judge man for who he is. The Bible says in 1 Peter 1:17 that God does not have respect toward people but judges every person according to how he lives. We read in 1 Corinthians 12:13 that by one spirit, we were all baptized into one body, whether Jews or Greeks, whether slaves or free. John tells us in Revelation 15:3, "Great and marvelous are Your works, Lord God Almighty! Just and true are Your ways." We are to live honestly, truthfully, justly, purely, and with love for other people. If we live godly, we will treat all people fairly and equally.

QUESTIONS FOR REFLECTION

1. Does the character of God that we examined in this chapter (good, kind, merciful, forgiving) match up with what you've understood of God throughout your life?
2. How has this examination of the character of God influenced your belief in whether God really exists?
3. What (or who) is your god?
4. If there is no god, why does man have questions about his future?

OUR FATHER WHO IS IN HEAVEN: IS GOD YOUR FATHER?

You are my Father, my God, and the rock of my salvation.
—PSALM 89:26

The Lord's Prayer, written in Matthew 6:9–13, is quoted by many people, but how many know what they are saying? God, "Our Father," is stated 261 times in the Bible. How many people say the Lord's Prayer from memory yet do not believe in God? God created man from the dust of the earth and breathed the breath of life into his nostrils. If God created us, does that make Him our Father?

Man knows he inherits certain traits from his parents. The Bible says in John 4:24 that God is a Spirit; He is not flesh. If God is Spirit and man is created in His image, how can we say our Father who is in heaven? Jesus Christ was flesh and blood while here on earth. The Bible gives us many references in the Book of John, saying Christ and God are one and the same. John 10:30 says, "I and My Father are one." Man will never understand how Jesus Christ was flesh and blood and God at the same time. Yet there is no doubt in my mind the Bible is true. Furthermore, Luke 18:27 says, "The things which are impossible with men are possible with God."

Jesus Christ was there when man was formed from the dust of the earth. The Bible says in Genesis 1:26, "Let Us make man in Our image." I believe every person was created physically like he is today because Genesis 1:12 says all life had its seed within itself. There was no transference of DNA from God to man, nor were there any genetic traits passed from Jesus' parents to Him. The Bible tells us in Luke 1:35 that Jesus was of God, not man. In Hebrews 7:3, we find Christ was without father or mother and did not have beginning of days nor end of life. But Christ was made in the likeness of men. Jesus Christ had earthly parents even though He was God. We recite the Lord's Prayer from memory. God is our heavenly Father, but He is not our physical father. In Genesis 5:1, we read that Adam was created in the likeness of God. All mankind is a descendant of Adam. Does man continue to have a likeness to his Creator? Do we have a heavenly Father?

The Bible asks us in Malachi 2:10, "Have we not all one Father? Has not one God created us?" Psalm 89:26 says, "You are my Father, my God, and the rock of my salvation." Ephesians 4:6 tells us God is the Father of all. The Bible says in 1 Corinthians 8:6 that there is one God and Father of all things. Even though man is not biologically connected to God, there is something in man that is uniquely from God alone. We read in Psalm 33:15 that God fashioned every man's heart. Solomon tells us in Proverbs 4:23 to keep our hearts strong, for out of it are the issues of life. Our physical hearts pump blood to all parts of our bodies, but our non-physical hearts are where all the issues of life flow. Biologically, we are descendants of our earthly parents; however, our hearts, souls, and spirits came from God. Ephesians 2:10 says, "For we are His workmanship, created in Christ Jesus for good works." God fit the body together to be a holy temple unto the Lord (Ephesians 2:21).

This physical body in which we live is just dust of the earth. The Bible says in James 2:26 that the body without the spirit is dead. The world will tell us man evolved over millions, possibly billions, of years. Man was created differently than anything else because he was precisely formed by God. The Bible says in 2 Peter 1:3 that according to God's divine power, He has given to man all things that pertain to life and godliness. Although God is not our biological father, He is our heavenly Father. This physical body in which we live is just dust and clay God molded to form us. In Ezekiel 37, God put life into a valley of dry, deteriorated bones. Genetically, we are descendants of our ancestors. But our real life is from God, our heavenly Father.

QUESTIONS FOR REFLECTION

1. What traits of God can you see in yourself as He created you?
2. If we are evolving, will we still be human in a million years?
3. Can you totally say that all of your characteristics are from your ancestors?

THE EARTH IS FILLED WITH THE KNOWLEDGE OF THE LORD

You have made known to me the ways of life.
—Acts 2:28

In everything that exists, God has revealed Himself to man. The Bible says in Numbers 14:21, "All the earth shall be filled with the glory of the LORD." In Psalm 19:1, we read, "The heavens declare the glory of God; and the firmament shows His handiwork." In Psalm 19:3, we see that creation speaks in all languages, and every person can hear the sound of God. In all the world and in the deepest part of man's soul, God is revealed. Psalm 104:24 tells us God's wisdom is seen in all creation, and the earth is full of His riches. Furthermore, we read in Romans 1:20, "For since the creation of the world His invisible attributes are clearly seen, being understood by the things that are made, even His eternal power and Godhead, so that they are without excuse."

Man claims to be knowledgeable, yet he will deny the existence of God. There is order in how everything functions in this world. But man believes everything somehow randomly came together and functions in an orderly manner.

The Bible says in the first chapter of Genesis that God created all things. In Genesis 1:14, we read that God placed the sun, moon, and stars in the sky for signs, seasons, days, and years. Before creation, there was no recorded history of time. Why is history dated BC and AD? BC is the era before Christ was born. AD is anno Domini, which is Latin for the year of the Lord. Recorded history will tell us Jesus Christ existed. Why does man want to throw God out of all public places, yet time revolves around Christ's existence?

The Nation of Israel also reveals God to every person. Israel was not formed by man but by God. The Bible says in Isaiah 43:15, "I am the LORD, your Holy One, the Creator of Israel, your King." Why does the whole world know about Israel? Every Christian has his heritage from the Jewish people, and Jesus Christ was born a Jew. The Bible and God's law were handed down to all people through the Jews. The world does not fear Israel, but *they fear the God of Israel*. Every person knows God, but every person wants to live in the dark, thinking his sinful nature cannot be seen. Man does not fear God, yet nations do!

The Bible gives us knowledge of God and reveals everything we need to know about life. We read in Psalm 19:7–8, "The law of the LORD is perfect, converting the soul; the testimony of the LORD is sure, making wise the simple; the statutes of the Lord are right, rejoicing the heart; the commandment of the Lord is pure, enlightening the eyes." God has revealed to man how he is supposed to live. Laws give man boundaries in which to live. If he stays within those boundaries, his soul will find rest; however, when man tries to live outside the law, he only finds confusion. The Bible says in Acts 2:28 that God has made known to man the ways of life. You may feel the Bible is nothing more than a law book. But it will take you down every road in life and show you what is at the end of each road.

Hebrews 8:10 says God has written His laws into man's mind and heart. Every person has a moral conscience and knows God's law. The Bible says in Ephesians 1:17 that Jesus Christ has given every person the spirit of knowledge to know Him. The Bible tells us everything that exists reveals God. The soul in man directly connects man to God; however, our souls will not give us a pass into heaven. Jesus told Nicodemus in John 3:3 that he had to be "born again," and Romans 1:20 tells us that no one will have an excuse.

QUESTIONS FOR REFLECTION

1. Science tells us that everything that exists in our universe evolved or came about by some massive explosion. Why does man try to explain such complex, intricate structure and design by claiming it was random?
2. What can you find in the natural world that attests to the idea of a master designer?
3. Does the complexity of the human body help you to see how evolution is far less likely than the master design of a Creator?

CREATED IN THE IMAGE AND LIKENESS OF GOD

Let Us make man in Our image and in Our likeness.
—GENESIS 1:26

What does it mean to be in the image of someone? *The American Heritage Dictionary of the English Language* defines image as a likeness of the appearance of something. It clearly resembles the original. Our heritage can be followed because man inherits characteristics from his ancestors; however, God is Spirit, and there can be no transference of DNA from God to man. How, then, can man be in the likeness of God? The Bible says in Psalm 33:15 that God fashioned all of mankind's hearts. Everything that encompassed Adam's soul exists in all human life today. Nothing has changed from the beginning, yet all human life is unique. Furthermore, the Bible says all life has seed within itself to reproduce its own likeness. If we evolved, why are we male and female?

THE STEPS OF MAN

Human beings were created to have relationships with God and other people. We were created for God's glory. Are there any animals that have lasting relationships? Is there anything in animal life that connects them to God? Do animals have a moral conscience? The Bible says in Deuteronomy

30:15, "I have set before you today life and good, death and evil." One thing is certain—you will die someday.

Jeremiah 7:24 says, "They did not obey or incline their ear, but followed the counsels and the dictates of their evil hearts." Jeremiah 7:19 says that man's sin provokes him to confusion. The Bible tells us the way of man is not in himself; he does not know how to direct his own steps. We have a free will to choose how we want to live. We can believe anything we want about life, but what is the basis of the choices we make?

LIKENESS: THE TRAITS OF REAL LIFE

The Bible tells us in Psalm 16:6 that man has a good heritage. God fashioned every person for His honor and glory. In Ephesians 2:10, we see man is God's workmanship created in Christ Jesus. He fashioned the parts of us that are vital to every action and feeling we have in our bodies. God is not our earthly father, but we are created in His image and likeness. When we describe the word image, we think of something physical. But when we describe the word likeness, it encompasses much more. Although God is a Spirit, Colossians 1:14–15 says Christ is the image of the invisible God. The Bible tells us in 1 John 3:2 that when Jesus appears, we will be like Him.

What do you know about His likeness? From cover to cover of the Bible, the likeness of God is revealed. Every person has a part of God's likeness in his soul. There are some characteristics of God that are exclusively of Him. The Bible says in Isaiah 6:3, "Holy, holy, holy is the LORD." In Psalm 145:17, we read, "The Lord is righteous in all His ways." Psalm 25:10 says, "All the paths of the LORD are mercy and truth." Jeremiah 4:2 says, "The Lord lives in truth, in judgment, and in righteousness." Furthermore, Psalm 104:2 says God is covered in light, and there is no darkness in Him. From these verses, we know people will never be like God. We can, however, be true and righteous if we allow Christ to live within us. The entire Bible tells us about God, but there are areas of His Word that allow man a closer look at God's likeness. Three of these areas are in Matthew 5:3–48 (the Beatitudes), Galatians 5:22–26 (the fruit of the Spirit), and Colossians 3:12—17 (character of the new man).

The Bible says in Galatians 5:22-23 that if we have the Spirit of God within our souls, we should have the fruit of love, joy, peace, longsuffering, gentleness, goodness, faith, meekness, and temperance manifested in how we live. A couple of chapters back, I wrote about the nature of God. Do you have any of these characteristics in the person you are? Proverbs 10:12 says love covers all sins. Jesus Christ died on the cross for the sins of all mankind, for He loved us. By God's nature, He manifests these qualities to man all the time. By design, every person has a part of God within himself in his soul.

The Bible tells us in Colossians 3:12–14 that we are to be kind, forgiving, forbearing, and humble. Are we kind people, warm and friendly to everyone we encounter? Kindness, forgiveness, and humility are characteristics of God. What about forbearance, which means to have tolerance and restraint? Abstinence and patience are other terms used to describe it.[54] How tolerant are we of the opinions of others? Today, it takes a lot of forbearance just to live with other people. Do people see kindness, humility, forgiveness and forbearance in the way we live?

Jesus tells us in Matthew 5 that blessed are they who are poor in spirit and those who mourn. Poorer people usually do not have as many barriers in seeking God and trusting in Him. When people mourn, they need some comfort for the loss they feel. Jesus tells us the meek are blessed. I have heard it said meekness is controlled strength. Patience and longsuffering are equated with meekness. Blessed are those who hunger for righteousness, for they shall be filled. Blessed are the merciful—do we have compassion and concern for other people? Blessed are those who are pure in heart. Pureness begins with God because sin does not want to be associated with Him. In Matthew 5:10, Jesus says, "Blessed are those who are persecuted for righteousness' sake." Living right before others begins with Jesus Christ.

---

[54] "Forbearance," *The American Heritage Dictionary of the English Language.*

Believers are to be salt and light to a world that has neither. John 1:5 says the light of Jesus shined in the darkness, but the darkness did not want the light. Evolution says the world we live in is progressing toward a better place, but I believe the world is getting darker every day we live.

There are many people in the world who do not believe in God; however, they will tell us they love people. The Bible is very plain in saying it is impossible for man to love anything but himself. In 1 John chapter 4, the Bible says if we can love others, God dwells in our souls. In verse 10, we read that man did not love God first, but God loved us and sent His Son to die for our sins. In verse 12, we see that no one has seen God at any time. If we love one another, God dwells in us. If we have any other virtues dwelling within our souls, they did not come from our mortal bodies.

If we look at all these attributes of God and look closely at man, a part of God's likeness is present in every person. The Bible says in John 1:4 that in Christ is life and that life is the light of men. We read in 1 Samuel 17:26 that He is the living God, and that is why man can have life. What is life to you? Is it just the physical beating of your heart and breathing? If that is all there is, life has no purpose or meaning. In God is life because He is the living God.

Mankind Uncovered

The Bible tells us in detail who God is and what man has become. Man thinks he is good. It is time to peel back the surface of man and get to the deepest part of his heart and soul. The Bible gives us a guided tour of exactly who we are. If we look in a mirror, we may turn in different ways to reveal our best appearance. There is nothing hidden; everything is naked before God. We may think we are pretty good people, but the light of God reveals everything about who we are. We may be able to talk our way out of our situation to other men, but Psalm 116:11 says, "All men are liars."

I have shared with you some of the character of mankind in the chapter "Who is Man?" Man cannot see himself, nor does he know he has a sin nature. Man lives in a world of deception, and he cannot see it. John 8:44

says the devil is a murderer and a liar, and he is the father of liars. Man often lives in the vanity and emptiness of his own mind.

Galatians, Colossians, and Romans are three books that tell about man's character. In these books, the Bible gives us a good description of what man has become. In Galatians 5:19–21, there are several terms used to describe people. Some of them you may not be familiar with, but I looked them up in the dictionary.[55] Verses 19–21 tell us that the works of the flesh of man manifest in adultery, fornication, uncleanness, lasciviousness, idolatry, witchcraft, hatred, variance, emulations, wrath, strife, sedition, heresies, envy, murder, drunkenness, reveling, and other like behaviors.

I am sure you have heard of some of these words. Adultery is defined as voluntary sexual intercourse between married people who are not married to each other. Fornication is sexual intercourse between unmarried people. Uncleanness is defined as someone who is foul, dirty, and morally defiled. Lasciviousness is a term you do not hear used much, but it is described as lustful, lewd, wanton, exciting sexual desires. Idolatry is the worship of idols; it is blind admiration or devotion to something man has created. Witchcraft is magic, sorcery, an influence, attraction, or charm that casts a spell on someone. Hatred is a violent dislike for someone. The word hate is used more now than at any time before in my life of seventy-six years. Variance is a term you may not be used to; it is a state in which you are different from what is expected; you dispute and disagree over what is considered the usual rule or law. Emulation is another term man does not use today. Emulation is man's effort or ambition to make himself better than another person or jealous rivalry. Do you have a desire to be better than everyone around you? Wrath is violent, resentful anger or rage. Strife is heated, often violent, disagreements or conflicts. Sedition is language inciting rebellion against authority. Heresy is an opinion or doctrine that goes against established religious beliefs, and it is controversial. Envy is a strong desire to have something that belongs to someone else. Murder is

---

[55] *The American Heritage Dictionary of the English Language.*

the unlawful killing of another person, usually with malice. Drunkenness is being intoxicated with a chemical to the point of impairment of physical and mental faculties. Revelry is boisterous merrymaking; it is a noisy festivity and sometimes shows rebellion.

Did you see anything in that list that reflects who you are? This is just a partial list of what man has become. In Colossians 3:5–9, the Bible lists more of the character of man. Some of the terms listed in these verses have already been listed and defined. These verses tell us man must mortify his body from inordinate affection, evil concupiscence, covetousness, disobedience, malice, blasphemy, filthy communication, and lying.

The American Heritage Dictionary of the English Language defines these words as well. Inordinate affection is exceeding reasonable limits; it is unrestrained affection. Evil concupiscence is evil sexual desires or lust with an abnormally strong desire. Covetousness is an excessive wishful desire to have something. Disobedience is the willful failure to follow directions or rules. Malice is the desire to harm others or see others suffer. Blasphemy involves the profane acts of man concerning God, claiming he has attributes of God. Filthy communication is the soiled or dirty exchange of obscene thoughts or messages, written or oral. Lying is the false, deliberate intent of presenting something which is not true. How often have you heard the term "fake news"?

The Bible tells us more about the character of man in the book of Romans. In Romans 1:21–32, we read that man is vain in his imaginations; his foolish heart is darkened; he professes to be wise but has become a fool; he has made God like any other lifeform; he is unclean through the desires of his heart; he dishonors his own body because of lusts; he changes truth into a lie; he worships idols instead of the Creator; he has changed his natural affection into that which is against nature; he is full of wickedness, unrighteousness, debate, deceit, malignity; he is a gossiper and backbiter; he hates God; he is despicable, a boaster; he invents evil things; he is disobedient to his parents; he is without understanding; he is a contract breaker; he is implacable and unmerciful.

What do these words mean to you? Romans 1:21 says man is vain in his imaginations. Vanity is described as being empty. In Genesis 6:5, we read that God saw the wickedness of man and that it was great in the earth and that every imagination of the thoughts of his heart was continually on evil. Man wants to keep his heart in the dark and live in darkness because his life is evil (John 3:19).

In the world in which we live, man no longer fears God, his Creator, because he does not honor his own body. The Bible says in Leviticus 19:28, "You shall not make any cuttings in your flesh nor print any marks on you: I am the LORD." In this day and time, does this verse apply to tattoos? In Romans 1:26–27, we see men and women have changed their natural use into that which is against nature. In Leviticus 20:13, the Bible says, "If a man lies with a male as he lies with a woman, both of them have committed an abomination." Man does not want to retain God in his heart. For this reason, God has given him over to a reprobate mind. Someone with a reprobate mind is a person who has no moral conscience. In Romans 1:29, we read that man is wicked. His wickedness is evident in vicious habits and mischievous, malicious, and harmful behaviors. His heart is filled with envy, murder, debate, deceit, malignity, and gossip. Debate is to argue about something and not discuss it. Malignity is an intense ill will with hate and great malice. It is a state of being highly evil, resulting in injury or death to someone.

In verses 29 to 30 of Romans 1, we see more of the character of man. He reveals himself as being a whisperer and backbiter, a hater of God, despiteful, a boaster, an inventor of evil things, disobedient to parents, a contract breaker, implacable, and without natural affection. A whisperer is someone who gossips, and a backbiter is someone who will lie about you behind your back. Man will try to remove God from any public place. The Bible says man hates God. Man will call out to God in one breath and will curse Him the next. Do you hate God? Are you despicable? A despicable person is someone who is full of malice; he is defiant. Do you like to boast or brag about who you are and your accomplishments? If you boast, you have a very high opinion of yourself; you have exalted yourself. Self-pride is an enemy of God. What is on your mind all the time? Do you have evil thoughts? Are you thinking about inventing or creating something evil? The people who want to kill a lot of people—is evil continually on their minds? The Bible says we will be disobedient to our parents. I continually see parental authority has little meaning anymore in society. It is no longer politically correct to discipline your children for disobedience.

In verse 31, we see man will be without understanding. It seems common sense no longer exists in everyday life. To understand means to perceive and comprehend the nature and significance of something. Discernment is also a part of understanding something. Do you agree to do something and then change your mind? When I was a child growing up, a handshake or someone's word was as good as any written contract. The Bible says people will be covenant or contract breakers. A contract is only as good as the people involved in signing it. The Bible tells us to be true and just in all we are. In verse 31, we read that man is implacable. Do you know the word or its meaning? Implacable means you are incapable of being pleasant. Do people like being around you? That verse also says man will be unmerciful. I know there are many people who are very generous and kind, but more and more people are becoming unlikable. Merciful means you are compassionate and caring.

God used another term to call mankind in Exodus 32:9. He said man is "stiff-necked." Stiff-necked means you are stubborn, unyielding, and obstinate. In Isaiah 65:2, we read man is rebellious. In Isaiah 53:6, the Bible says man has gone his own way; every one has gone astray. Every person sins and has no fear of God. People see God's love but not His judgment. In man's self-righteousness, he sees a God who will let all sin go without condemnation. The Bible says in Proverbs 10:23 that it is a sport or game to a fool to sin and commit mischief.

This list of terms the Bible uses to describe man is not all-inclusive; man's behavior is described from cover to cover in the Bible. These terms tell us the deep, hidden nature of man's heart. You may feel you are a good person, but our Creator knows exactly who you are. God knows the evil imaginations of every person's heart. You hear politicians say they are going to be transparent. Most people will never be transparent to you and me, but they are before God.

OBEDIENT: WILLING TO BE USED

Every person is fashioned by a living God. We live in a time in which people want to know who they are. They do not know whether they are male or female. The Bible tells us in James 1:13 that God does not tempt mankind with evil. If you are confused, Satan has you where he wants you to be. He is the great deceiver and father of lies. You may be asking, "Why am I different? If we were created in the image of God, why am I this way?" Do you feel you should be of the opposite sex from which you were born? I do not know why some people are born different or with physical problems. The Bible says God's ways are higher than man's. We will never know the why of the question. In Isaiah 43:7, the Bible says man was created for God's glory.

We were specifically fashioned by our Creator for His purpose. Man looks at himself and bases who he is on his strength and his abilities. He will idolize someone for their athletic skills, talents, and other visible attributes. They are highly visible in society and receive attention from everyone. Because of their stature and recognition in the public, they are seen as the ideal role model. They are put on a pedestal to be idolized.

The Bible says in Psalm 147:10 that God does not delight in the strength of a horse, nor does He need man's legs. God asks Moses in Exodus 4:11, "Who has made man's mouth? Or who makes the mute, the deaf, the seeing, or the blind?" Man sees his greatest assets in his legs (strength). His mouth represents every other quality he has. Everything man sees as essential for being someone is not important to God. The Bible says in 1 Samuel 16:7 that the Lord does not see as man does, for man looks on the outward appearance, but God looks on man's heart. Man will look at his limitations; God sees His purpose in creating each of us. We see our problems, never thinking everything is possible with God. The Bible says in Colossians 2:10 that we are complete in Christ, who is the head of all principality and power. If we give our hearts to God, there are no limits to what He can do with us. No person will ever be complete apart from God. It is God who makes us whole. Our purpose was never based on our physical bodies; it was based upon our hearts and souls.

You may be thinking if I was like such a person, I would be somebody. The greatest person I have known of in my lifetime did not win any championships in sports. He was not a movie star, nor did he have great talent or wealth. The media did not put him on a pedestal to be idolized. Yet he was probably seen by more people all over the world than anyone. He probably touched more lives than any person you and I will ever know. That person was Billy Graham. He allowed God to use him, and he reached out to people everywhere he went. The Bible says in Philippians 2:13 that it is God who works in us for His will and good pleasure. Children not yet born have a purpose with Him. Our limitations are unlimited possibilities with Him. Every one of us was created for His honor and glory. Greatness to God is for you and me to give our hearts to Him. If we humble ourselves before God, He will lift us up. The love, peace, and joy we seek in life are not found in people or things. It is found in our souls in Jesus Christ. Every person is different because we are created specifically for God's purpose. There is no one else like you and me. We are complete in Him.

WHO ARE YOU

I have given you the characteristics of God and man. Did you make a list and see who you most closely resemble? Man wants to compare himself to others, but God is the standard. The Bible tells us *all* mankind sins. How are you measuring up to holiness, righteousness, purity, and truth? The Bible says God knows your thoughts and the intent of your heart. What are you going to do when you cannot lie or hide?

The Bible says in James 1:17 that every good and perfect gift is from above and comes down from God. Do you still feel self-righteousness about yourself? I have given you the character of the heart of every person born of woman. Jeremiah 17:9 says, "The heart is deceitful above all things, and desperately wicked; who can know it?" The Bible tells us exactly who we are. Romans 1:32 says man knows the righteous judgment of God, and he knows the sins he commits are worthy of death. But he continues to sin, and he takes pleasure in his sins. You may deny the existence of God and try to remove Him from your mind and your world; however, you cannot remove Him from your soul. Every good thing about you and me that manifests itself to others is from God. Solomon tells us in Ecclesiastes 12:7 that when we die, our bodies will return to the dust from which they came, and our spirits will return to God, who gave them life.

God created you and me in His image and likeness, and the Bible says in Psalm 139:14, "I am fearfully and wonderfully made."

QUESTIONS FOR REFLECTION

1. If we are evolving, the next generation will be better than this one. Why, then, do we idolize anyone? Why is anyone a role model?
2. When you look at the things that make you who you are, what good and bad things come to mind? Are you closer to resembling man or God?
3. How do you truly want others to see you?

IT IS WRITTEN: NOTHING IS HID, THERE IS NO MYSTERY

I will give them a heart to know Me, that I am the Lord.
—JEREMIAH 24:7

Jesus tells us in Matthew 4:4, "It is written, 'Man shall not live by bread alone, but by every word that proceeds from the mouth of God.'" Everything that pertains to the life of man can be found in the Bible. Evolution says you are always progressing, changing from lower to higher and advancing from simple to more complex forms. There has always been detail, order, and purpose in God's creation. With man's way of doing things, is there order or chaos?

The Bible tells us in Isaiah 49:1 that from the womb, God has made known your name. If you look in the Bible in Genesis chapter 5, you will find the genealogy of Adam. If you look at the first eight chapters of 1 Chronicles, you will see the genealogy of all of Israel. Furthermore, Matthew chapter 1 and Luke chapter 3 tell us the genealogy of Jesus Christ. Why would all these people be listed by name if we evolved? Every person listed was somebody showing us they were important. If you evolved, you are nothing more than a speck in time. In the Bible, every person that was written about had a purpose.

When God gave man instructions to do something, He was very detailed. When the tabernacle and the temple were built, God was very explicit in how everything was to be constructed and placed. You will not find anywhere in the Bible that events happened by chance.

Solomon tells us in Ecclesiastes chapter 2 that the sum total of all that man strives to attain in life. He did not withhold anything from his eyes. In everything he tried to do and attain, he found it was all empty and worthless without God. In everything his eyes desired to have, he found nothing satisfied his soul. In that part of you where God put your soul, what are you trying to place there that is fulfilling?

EVERY PERSON KNOWS

Jeremiah 31:33 says God has put His laws into man's heart and mind. Within the soul of man, there is knowledge about God. In Jeremiah 24:7 we read, "I will give them a heart to know Me, that I am the LORD." First Corinthians 2:12 says that we have not received the spirit of the world but the Spirit of God, that we may know the things of Him. With that knowledge comes choices. Man will choose eternal life or eternal separation from Him in hell. The Bible says in Joshua 24:15, "Choose for yourselves this day whom you will serve." Every person gets to decide where he will spend eternity.

The Bible says in Isaiah 59:12 that our transgressions are multiplied before us, and we know it. Jesus tells us in John 8:32, "You shall know the truth, and the truth will make you free." But man does not want truth. He wants to live in the vanity of his foolish heart. The light of the world came to earth and shined in the darkness, but man does not want the light. The Bible says in Titus 2:11, "The grace of God that brings salvation has appeared to all men."

The Bible says in Psalm 19:1, "The heavens declare the glory of God, and the firmament shows His handiwork." Our eyes can see and our hearts reveal God to us. The Bible says in Romans 1:17 that the righteousness of God is revealed to every person. In verse 18, we see, "For the wrath of

God is revealed from heaven against all ungodliness and unrighteousness of men, who suppress the truth in unrighteousness." Nothing is hid; there are no mysteries—everything we need to know about life has been revealed or shown to us by God.

We all have the answers, yet mankind never learns. Why did Adam and Eve rebel against God? Why does the United States want to remove God from every public place in America? God has all the right answers, yet man does not want Him. God has given us His likeness, but man wants to walk in the darkness. The Bible says in Job 21:14, "Depart from us, for we do not desire the knowledge of Your ways." We read in Zechariah 7:11–12, "They refused to heed, shrugged their shoulders, and stopped their ears so they could not hear. Yes, they made their hearts like flint, refusing to hear the law and the words which the LORD of hosts has sent by His Spirit." Jesus tells us in Matthew 13:15, " For the hearts of this people have grown dull. Their ears are hard of hearing, and their eyes they have closed, lest they should see with their eyes and hear with their ears, lest they should understand with their hearts and turn, so that I should heal them." However, Romans 1:28 says men do not want to retain God in their knowledge. God told Moses in Exodus 32:9 that people are stiff-necked. In every area of life, God has made Himself known to man, but man rebels against everything that pertains to Him. Man wants to remove God from his mind and sight. He is either deceived or he has not discovered the soul in his physical body is from God. There will always be a struggle between his flesh and his soul.

Is the heart of man so wicked he rebels against God, or is he so deceived he can no longer see Him? Satan was in the Garden of Eden with Adam and Eve. All that existed at the time was God, creation, man, Satan, and Paradise. For man, that changed to deception, rebellion, and death. God tells us the wages of sin is death (Romans 6:23). In Genesis 3:4, Satan tells Adam and Eve they will not die if they sin. Why is it that they believed Satan but did not believe God? The Bible says in Isaiah 44:20 that a deceived heart has turned him away that he cannot deliver his own soul. We read in Romans 7:11 that sin deceives us, and by it, we are slain.

When we throw God out of our lives, we are turning off light at the same time. Maybe the reason man thinks he is a good person is because he has lived in the dark so long that he cannot see his true nature. The Bible tells us in 1 John 1:8, "If we say we have no sin, we deceive ourselves, and the truth is not in us." People can be deceived in many ways. Jesus tells us in Revelation 3:17, "You say, 'I am rich, have become wealthy, and have need of nothing'—and do not know that you are wretched, miserable, poor, blind, and naked." People will strive to attain everything they can get in life, thinking it will fill that part of them that came from God. That part that came from God is the sum total of who we are. Everything else about us returns to the dust from which it came. People are like sheep; they are led, not driven. Do you believe you can live your life the way you want and still go to heaven?

THE SUM TOTAL: MAN'S REBELLION AGAINST GOD

God gave every person a moral compass to know Him. That compass will guide us in the right direction, but it will not make us go that way. The Bible says it is not in man to know where he is going. Man has not learned that the farther he walks away from God, the darker the road gets. The only true light you and I have to see in this dark world is within our souls.

Everything we need to know about life is written in the Bible. The Bible says in 2 Timothy 3:15, "From childhood you have known the Holy Scriptures, which are able to make you wise for salvation through faith which is in Christ Jesus." Romans 15:4 says the Bible was written for our learning that we, through patience and comfort of the Scriptures, can have hope. We read in Daniel 9:13, however, that all this evil has come upon us because we have not turned from our wicked ways. From God and the Bible, we know we must choose every day between good and evil.

We know all creation came forth by design. Man, by his own deceived and rebellious heart, seeks to know things by looking at creation. When he begins to look at his Creator, he will be able to see some of the answers. Our knowledge and goodness came from God. *However, man has willfully and deliberately chosen to remove God from his heart and mind.* God has given us the knowledge to know truth. The Bible tells us we are all without excuse.

When God breathed the breath of life into me, I became a living soul. The Bible says in Psalm 139:7, "Where can I go from Your Spirit? Or where can I flee from Your presence?" The God who fashioned me is everywhere I am. God told Moses in Numbers 14:11 that He showed the people signs to know Him. God has given man everything we need to know about Him; we don't have any excuses. The Bible says in Psalm 17:15, "As for me, I will see Your face in righteousness; I shall be satisfied when I awake with your likeness." Do you want to be like Jesus Christ? If you are a born-again Christian, the Bible says one day, you will be like Him.

God did not create you and me with a blank slate in our souls. Genesis 1:26 says, "Let Us make man in Our image, according to Our likeness." From Adam and Eve until now, nothing has changed in God's design for mankind. Isaiah 59:21 reads: "'This is My covenant with them: My Spirit who *is* upon you, and My words which I have put in your mouth, shall not depart from your mouth, nor from the mouth of your descendants, nor from the mouth of your descendants' descendants,' says the LORD, 'from this time and forevermore.'" Every person was created by God and for Him and His glory. The Bible says every person knows God. There are no places to hide, nor can man remove Him from his soul. Deep down in your soul, you know about God—everybody does. The Bible tells us you know, and you don't have any excuses.

QUESTIONS FOR REFLECTION

If you have questions or feel confused, God is not far away if you seek Him. "And He has made from one blood every nation of men to dwell on all the face of the earth, and has determined their preappointed times and the boundaries of their dwellings, so that they should seek the Lord, in the hope that they might grope for Him and find Him, though He is not far from each one of us" (Acts 17:26–27).

RESOURCES

The Thompson Chain-Reference Bible, Fifth Edition, and the *Thomas Nelson New King James Bible* were my Scripture sources throughout this book.

Matthew Henry's Commentary, (Grand Rapids, Michigan: Zondervan, 1961).

John Gill, "John Gill's Exposition of the Bible," *Bible Study Tools*, https://www.biblestudytools.com/commentaries/gills-exposition-of-the-bible/.

> *I used these two commentaries for Scripture emphasis in the first few chapters only. From that point to the conclusion, I relied on the Spirit of God to direct my thoughts on what I wanted to convey to the readers.

The Strongest Strong's Exhaustive Concordance of the Bible (Grand Rapids, Michigan: Zondervan, 2001).

ABOUT THE AUTHOR

Roger Richey grew up on a farm in rural Northeast Arkansas, one of twelve children. He learned to work at an early age because cotton was the main source of their livelihood. From humble beginnings, he would serve in the US Air Force and later pursued postgraduate education. He retired from work as a family nurse practitioner in 2016. His education gave him many opportunities in life, but it did not present Jesus Christ to him. Through family, friends, and a small country church, however, he became a Christian.

Being a Christian does not remove anyone from the heartaches of life. His first wife died of cancer when their daughter was twelve years old. He is married again and has two other stepsons. His biggest goal now in life is to read through the Bible every year. This is his fourteenth straight year, and it has been very revealing. The Bible lives, and that is why it holds a special place in his heart.

"Through reading the Bible, God has spoken to me, and I hope He will speak to you when you read this book."

www.ingramcontent.com/pod-product-compliance
Lightning Source LLC
Chambersburg PA
CBHW061152120626
46546CB00005B/2024